Sheila

Best wishes

to you.

Dave

Defining, Designing and Launching

M.A.P.

(Market Aimed Products)

A Revolutionary Process For Developing New
Products For the 21st Century

by DAVE BIGGS

Preface by DAVE GARWOOD

Defining, Designing and Launching
MAP
(Market Aimed Products)

by Dave Biggs
Preface by Dave Garwood

Dogwood Publishing Company, Inc.
501 Village Trace, Bldg. 9A
Marietta, GA 33067
(800) 368-7775

Defining, Designing and Launching
MAP
(Market Aimed Products)

© 1995, Dogwood Publishing Company, Inc.
501 Village Trace, Bldg. 9A
Marietta, GA 33067
(800) 368-7775

First Printing

Text and editing by Michael Bane

ISBN 0-9621118-8-0

Contents

Preface
by Dave Garwood

Unfolding The MAP

What is MAP all about? In essence, it is increasing your batting average with new products and spending less time and money doing it.

Product quality has become a given, almost a commodity. Competition has sent a clear message: Defect-free products or services won't be enough to differentiate a company from the competition and lead the industry. The leaders will differentiate themselves by lowering costs to deliver higher value to the customer. They will also be frequently bringing innovative ideas to their customers with a steady stream of new products. Product life cycles will get increasingly shorter. Speed will be key to survival.

This book is about how to significantly raise the quality, speed and effectiveness of your new product development process. This book is different from anything you have previously read on this subject—I guarantee you will learn how to develop new products from a totally new perspective.

Most books on new product development have focused on concurrent engineering, that is, developing products and processes simultaneously. Which is an excellent concept; necessary, but not sufficient. Other books have focused on strategy or marketing tools. This book is about a proven process that ties all the concepts together. With MAP, a company CEO can guarantee that the new product development process executes the corporate strategy.

Nor is the MAP process another untried theory. The process is currently being used very successfully to develop new products at the Bently Nevada Corporation, and MAP has served them well. They've increased new products as a per cent of sales from 10% to over 40% in a relatively short time. They've doubled the number of new products introduced each year without increasing the size of the Engineering staff. Product quality has simultaneously increased significantly.

I have had the privilege of working with Bently Nevada Corporation for over 15 years. In many ways, Bently Nevada is an unusual organization. They have been blessed with exceptionally strong executive leadership. Don Bently, Chairman and Founder, and Roger Harker, President, constantly challenge the organization to search for a better way. The entire organization has a constant thirst for new ideas and does not allow historical success to blind them to new opportunities. They have a bias for action throughout the organization. They maintain an atmosphere that encourages individuals to experiment without fear of failure. They thrive on competition from the Pacific Rim—and usually win. These are a few of the characteristics of this World Class organization that nurtured the evolution of MAP.

Dave Biggs, Senior Vice President at Bently Nevada, has taken the last few years to learn, adjust and refine MAP. He has also listened to the problems and solutions with new product development efforts in many other companies with varied product lines. During this same period, he has been the hands-on-executive using MAP to convert company strategy to deliverable products at Bently Nevada. This book represents not only "best practices" from many companies, but a process that has passed the acid test in today's challenging real world.

Dave has done a superior job of transforming the practices at Bently Nevada into a well-defined process—MAP—that is applicable to any manufacturing or service business. Many old new product development paradigms are challenged and discarded. New product development is viewed as a business process that cuts horizontally across traditional business functions. Dave, with the help of Michael Bane, explains in clear, easy-to-understand business English how to re-engineer your new product development process and raise the quality of the results. They address head-on many of the tough detail issues, such as how to get a complete definition before design begins, how to manage costs and avoid unpleasant surprises, how to measure the effectiveness of the process, how to select the right team leader and many more.

This book is must reading for companies genuinely serious about raising and meeting their customers expectations faster than their competitors. This book is your MAP to the future.

Chapter 1

Introduction

Here's a short story that might make you wince...

The plastic box sat inert on the polished wooden surface of the conference room table. The box was neither the expected computer gray or spilt-coffee brown. Instead, it was a muted teal color, with a bright yellow logo in the upper left corner of the face. Three people circled the table like nervous animals, clearly too agitated to stop moving, much less sit.

"All I want to know is where I plug these in," said the taller of the two men. He was dressed in Brooks Brothers business armor, right down to the regimental tie. Incongruously, he held a set of yellow Sony stereo earphones at the end of his outstretched arm. "Because if I can't plug these in, we are in some deep...well...trouble."

"Cute, Tom," answered the only woman in the room. Amanda Jakes, the head of Engineering, was rapidly running out of whatever good humor remained. "You know there's no place to plug earphones into this CD drive. That was never on our final specs..."

"It was, however, on our contract with Golden Moon," Tom Williams, the director of Sales/Marketing, countered. "How

could this have happened?"

"That's a fair question," said the third man, running his hand through graying hair. At 53 years-old Dave Jones had the reputation of being a high-tech wizard. His products littered Silicon Valley, and as CEO of FutureEDGE, Inc., he presided over a public offering that was nothing short of phenomenal. The plastic box on the table was supposed to not only enhance that reputation, but put dollars in the pockets of all those shareholders. The X-15 CD-ROM drive was faster than even NEC's latest. It was also smaller, greener—able to reap the public relations benefits of capturing the Energy Star label—and, Jones smiled to himself, cooler looking than all those little industrial beige boxes.

It was also 12 months late, 65 percent over budget and now this. He looked at his two vice presidents and shook his head. What a screw-up! Part of the driving force behind the development of the X-15 had been the huge order from Golden Moon in Korea, who liked the idea of one-upping Sony and NEC on this one. The problem was that the Korean order had specified a jack for stereo headphones, common on most computer CD players. Somewhere in the rush to market, that jack had vanished.

"There's more," said Jakes, obviously reluctant. "If we re-engineer for the jacks, we've got a wholesale problem with the case and the main board..." She gestured to the teal box... "Things are damn tight in there."

Jones rubbed his head. Twelve months late to market; Apple, for heaven's sake, had already dropped their faster unit, and it looked like a miniature mothership. The trade papers were full of "The end of the industrial box" stories. Stories that should have been about us, he thought.

"I've also heard of some quality problems with the drive itself," Jones added.

"It's not running to speed," Jakes said promptly. "We think it's component problems. What's coming off the line isn't matching what we've come to expect in the prototype boxes. We're still working on it."

"If we don't do a major push, we can kiss the market goodbye," said Williams. "All this publicity about CD-ROMs, the

Information Highway, all that stuff isn't going to last. We're playing catch-up as it is."

"We're getting nowhere beating each other," Jones said, cutting short Jakes' reply. "But I want that first questioned answered: how did this happen? Is it going to happen on our next launch? Because, if it does, this company is in serious trouble."

Walking out of the office, Tom was conciliatory.

"I'm sorry, Amanda, but I just got hammered long distance from Korea. I didn't mean to beat you over the head with it."

"We designed what we were told to design—I know, I know. It's not what we needed to sell," she said. "This isn't the first, you know. Only the worst."

"What do you mean?"

"Seems like we start out every design cycle all pumped up, with these great intentions," she started, "and end up in a conference room, assigning blame and killing off the wounded."

"Yeah," Tom agreed. "Unfortunately, that's true. How are we going to salvage this one?"

"Good question."

When she got back to her office, the engineering team for X-15 was waiting for her.

"The damn jacks were eliminated along about the tenth revision," said the senior engineer, Jo Allison, before Jakes could even speak. "We designed what we were told to design."

"And redesigned it and redesigned it and redesigned it," added one of the engineering team.

Jakes slumped down in her seat and stared at a three-dimensional representation of the drive on her workstation.

"This ought to really make your day," Jo Allison added. "Manufacturing has been calling all day griping about a couple of our tolerances we've spec'ed. They're saying they can't hold them when we crank up the main line—not without a major equipment overhaul. They want to know how come we didn't design something they could build."

"Just for once, couldn't they build something we designed?" she said, but her heart wasn't in it...

* * *

If new product development really is the lifes' blood of a company, why do we do such a bad job of it?

Because that is the reality.

Despite almost a decade of altering, twisting, fine-tuning our new product development process, too many companies complain that their new products are late to market, over-budget, don't perform as billed, are difficult to manufacture, cost too much and don't come anywhere close to meeting the early preprototype expectations. Take a look at this list of symptoms of problems in the new product development process. Do any of them look familiar to you?

Symptoms of POOR New Product Development Process

- Late to market
- Excessive development costs
- Losing marketshare
- Low success rate
- Customers don't buy
- Playing "catch up" ball
- Sold before designed
- Excessive manufacturing costs
- Difficult to produce
- Suppliers can't perform
- Many engineering change orders
- Difficult to service
- Obsolete inventory
- Products don't work
- Massive fingerpointing
- Missing features and functions
- Early design decisions cause problems
- Frequently repeat mistakes
- BFO often next new product

Our question is the same one as CEO Jones in our mythical FutureEDGE company: how did this happen?

After all, it's not as if the new product development process hasn't been under intense scrutiny. Haven't we all studied the concepts of concurrent engineering? Isn't the idea of involving our suppliers—who are our partners, remember—early in the design process virtually a litany? Haven't we read the books on shortening our development cycle, taken seminars to help us become customer-centered, even gone so far as introducing our Manufacturing Engineers to our Design Engineers?

All this is not to say that we haven't gotten better. But as the vice president of new product development for a high-tech firm and a consultant on new product development, I have concluded that the results are far below what we expected in proportion to the dollars spent and the time invested.

How can this happen?

And, more importantly, can we stop this loss of time and money from continuing to happen?

Yes, we can.

We can accomplish this feat without spending a fortune on new software and the hardware to run it. We don't have to form a "SWAT" team or even hire a new vice-president. What it takes to stop this hemorrhaging is a willingness to examine our old new product development processes and tools, and make the changes we know are necessary.

MAP provides the outline and the tools necessary to revolutionize your new product development process. MAP—market-aimed products—are just that, new products that have been created to meet specific market needs. We've all given at the very least lip service to "creating products for the market." But what, exactly, does that phrase really mean? And how to we do it? The MAP process provides those answers and much more. For our new products to succeed, that phrase has to mean "creating products that solve our customers problems." People buy solutions to problems; in order to create new products that are successful, we have to have a gut-level understanding of what customer problems our products solve.

The MAP process gives you the tools to do exactly that.

At its most basic, the MAP process provides a template that takes you, step-by-step, from identifying those customer problems to launching the finished new product. We break the overall process down into five distinct sections, called phases, separated by go/no-go points called gates. The phases and gates concept isn't new; what is new, though, is codifying those phases into five sections—not three, not 22, as one hapless company ended up with. These five phases provide all the control you need without imposing a complex bureaucratic structure that hampers the easy flow of ideas. Our gates provide you with a clear understanding of the go/no-go decision—what has to happen—at each point.

Secondly, the MAP process provides a "toolkit" to help "install" MAP in your organization. There are tools to help you create a new product development review board to man the gates; tools to help you understand where your products are in their life cycles; tools to help you separate your customers' wants from their true needs. MAP also includes tools for accurately measuring the cost of both the new products and the process to create that product. Finally, there are additional tools for measuring how well the MAP process is working within your company.

We're going to be touching on some familiar subjects— concurrent engineering, supplier involvement, closeness to customers—and some unfamiliar ones—silos, S-curves, and scenario development. The key thing to remember, though, is that within the MAP process, each of these ideas and concepts have a specific place or a specific use. The MAP process has been used for products as varied as electronic measuring and consumer magazines. Whether the product is a truck, a computer or a service, MAP works.

Chapter 2

Stuck Under A Paradigm

Before we can explore the nuts and bolts of the MAP process, it's important to understand the business landscape that has necessitated such a sweeping change in the way we do business.

For people involved in the new product development process, the challenges are substantial (and, at times, daunting). Part of the problem is that the new challenges are easy to state in the abstract, but very hard to deal with in practice.

Simply stated, the challenges are to develop new products:
• That customers will purchase
• That can be developed quickly and efficiently
• That are manufacturable
• That are compatible with laws and regulations
• That do not cause a legal liability

The challenges are also accompanied by a changing landscape.

What has changed are both the rules of the game and the playing field itself. The competition has changed: The consumers are more demanding, the pace of technology has sped up, and government intervention and regulation have increased. The results of those changes have totally rewritten the concepts of new product development. Remember Henry Ford's concept for car colors? You could have any color you want, as long as it was black! Imagine that statement today. Nope, the new world is every color in the palette, mixed to your specifications. Consider the speed at which we routinely accept "technological miracles." Fax machines and cellular telephones rocketed into widespread acceptance. Schoolchildren routinely check onto the Internet to talk to friends and interview rock stars. And consider the changes wrought by environmental laws.

The fact is this: companies that understand the new rules are gaining tremendous advantage!

For us to understand the power of rules and why changing them is difficult, it's helpful to use the concept of paradigms.

The concepts of paradigms, originally formulated by Thomas Kuhn in his study of scientific breakthroughs, has recently been studied, refined and taught by futurist Joel Arthur Barker. The paradigm concept has also been used extensively by consultant Dave Garwood to evaluate and define (or redefine) the changing business environment.

A paradigm is best defined as a view, an outlook, a perception that includes a set of rules and regulations that defines boundaries and behavior to succeed within those boundaries. Paradigms are helpful in that they help us know how to succeed.

Paradigms do, however, have a dark side. When their rules no longer are able to help us solve our problems, we tend to cling to them anyway, because they succeeded in the past. For example, our factories still focus on "driving down" and obsessively measuring direct labor, even though direct labor costs are now only a fraction of the actual cost of the product. Or we still think in terms "mass markets" even our own experience tells us those mass markets are the dinosaurs of our time.

The old paradigm, then, serves as a filter, essentially allowing us to see only what we expect to see.

As pointed out by Barker, it is usually an outsider that has no vested interest in the existing paradigm who "discovers" the new paradigm that will solve the problems not effectively dealt with by the old rule set.

The Old Paradigm

Let's take a look at the old—or, unfortunately, existing—paradigm for new product development. Under that paradigm, products are developed through a series of activities. These activities are functionally oriented, that is, the project is handed off from department to department as it progresses through the process.

Which department puts the ball in play, so to speak, depends on how we view ourselves as a company. If we view ourselves as a marketing-driven company, the Marketing Department decides what the new product will be and then passes the product definition to Engineering. Engineering designs the product and hands the design off to Manufacturing. Manufacturing then tries to make the product manufacturable, and Materials Management begins to coordinate the logistics of the manufacturing process.

Right about when Materials Management began working, Marketing got its first glimpse of the real product, which usually held several nasty surprises for them. The results frequently were panic, revisions, redesigns and, in general, wasted resources.

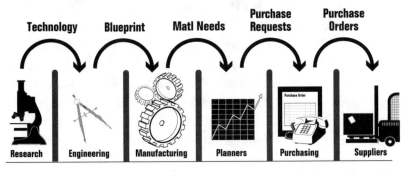

Product Development
Old Paradigm: Relay Race

| Technology | Blueprint | Matl Needs | Purchase Requests | Purchase Orders |

| Research | Engineering | Manufacturing | Planners | Purchasing | Suppliers |

This is a classic example of what we call the "silo effect." Silos are not only those tall structures filled with grain that dot the Great Plains. They're also how we view our company's functional departments. Engineering is a silo; Manufacturing is a silo; Sales is a silo. Silos have a way of becoming "companies within companies," with the objective being to maximize performance of the silo rather than the company. By their nature, silos restrict communications. The main reason for this critical constriction is that our loyalty is to our silo. When something goes wrong, we blame the other silo. This parochialism is death to communications, which is especially unfortunate, because business processes are horizontal rather than vertical! Our processes that deliver products or services to our customers cut across the silos. The new product development process is no different; it cuts across the silos. Every time the new product development process crossed into a new silo, the communication process took a fierce hit.

If we view ourselves as a technology-driven company, the process starts when Engineering announces they have the "solution" (any solution will do), and Marketing and Sales are told to find a market. The "solution" is turned into a design, then handed off to Manufacturing. Manufacturing hands the product to Marketing. The flow of the process is a little different, but the results are about the same—a long series of steps, with lots of friction between the departments, which frequently failed.

You'll notice that in this process, people outside the company aren't included in the early phases of the development process.

Unfortunately, one of the outsiders most frequently left out is the customer. It's amazing, how often the customer isn't involved, or involved only in trivial, pandering ways. We've spent millions of dollars building facilities to simulate the customers' situations, rather than developing effective ways to get the real customers involved in the process.

Suppliers are also left out. We design the component parts and practice the "put it out for bid and keep it cheap" supplier relations approach. The "relationship" with the suppliers is limited to the buyers in Purchasing, and their expertise is often ignored. The only "input" we want from our suppliers is their products.

Under the old paradigm, there's a lot of talk about "teamwork," which is defined as an absence of conflict. We see our coworkers as competition or obstacles. And problems with the process are usually blamed on other people in the organization.

The old paradigm/process has a way of backing people into corners, where it's very convenient to blame people in other organizations or silos for the problems. The classic corner is unrealistic deadlines, which encourages finger-pointing. The system of hand-offs often encourages inter-silo warfare, when the department who "got the ball" finds out they can't meet an unrealistic deadline for product design or that they have to meet a sales quota for a product that nobody seems to want to buy.

> The very phrase "concurrent engineering" once again suggests that new product development is the fiefdom of a single silo, Engineering.

The bottom line is that the old paradigm yielded new products, but the success rate—our batting average—wasn't particularly high. And the side-effects of the old process—the inter-silo warfare, long development time, interdepartmental distrust, cost overruns, finger-pointing—constantly chewed away at both the efficiency of the process and the productivity of the company as a whole.

To an extent, the focus on "concurrent engineering" as a solution to our new product development woes are part and parcel of that old paradigm. While the move to perform developmental activities concurrently is a good one—and one we'll be discussing at length later—the very phrase "concurrent engineering" once again suggests that new product development is the fiefdom of a single silo, Engineering. While this may not have been the intent of many of the good people working on concurrent engineering, it is the reality. What we really need is to think in terms of "concurrent new product development," which precisely defines the MAP process.

Earthquake!

To talk about the "shifting business landscape" does the actual upheaval a disservice. The shifting is more akin to a major earthquake, shaking the very foundations of the product development process.

The changes began a long time before most of us realized they were happening, and they've been steadily increasing in frequency and impact. It's only been in the last few years that Corporate America has begun to take the threat seriously. Part of the problem was that we failed to really understand why our global competition was killing us.

Our focus on business was on labor negotiations, price increases, mergers and acquisitions. When we focused on the production process, the emphasis was on mass production techniques, economies of scale. Yet we have seen the mass market fragment in a million smaller, "niche" markets, what has been called the "sneakerization" of markets. Remember sneakers? When we were in high school years ago, we had a pair of sneakers, canvas and rubber casual shoes. When we did athletic events, we usually wore our sneakers. Now, instead of that pair of sneakers, we have running shoes, walking shoes, basketball shoes, racquetball shoes, tennis shoes, bicycling shoes, aerobic shoes, step-aerobic shoes, wrestling shoes.

Product life-cycles are shrinking—it doesn't matter whether that product is an athletic shoe or a piece of heavy machinery or a computer or a financial service. At the same time, our customers are becoming increasingly demanding. As the burger commercial states, today's customers want to have it their way. And they will have it their way, either from you or from your competition. And that customization can't come at the expense of quality or for a higher price. In fact, today's customers want higher quality, and a lower price. We are moving helter skelter away from mass production to mass individualization, production in a lot size of one.

Management guru Tom Peters puts it well and simply: "Every market is splintering, and then splintering again. There are no non-niche markets anymore. So long, mass market."

The implications for the new product development process are staggering. We already knew we had to shorten those cycle times, get the product out quicker, with higher quality. But the truth is that we're going to have to have more products in the pipeline, and we're going to have to be able to make those products for a lower cost, because our margins are being squeezed.

In order to do all those things, we have to change the new product development paradigm.

Chapter 3

The New Vision

Yes, we are going to have to deal with "that vision thing" before we go on. It's become fashionable to discount even the word "vision" as not the kind of subject that a hard-nosed pragmatist-type CEO should fret about. Unfortunately, despite all this tough talk, it's a little hard to figure out where you're going without something that resembles a vision. A sequence in "Through The Looking Glass" comes to mind, where Alice asked the Mad Hatter where a particular road went. The Hatter asked where Alice wanted to go; she responded that it didn't matter. At which, the Hatter answered, "It doesn't matter which road you take, then." If we don't know where we're going, it's hard to plan how to get there.

Joel Arthur Barker refers to vision as, "dreams in motion," and that is not a bad definition. A vision can come from one individual, or it can be collectively arrived at by many people. One thing is true, though—there is a lot of value in the process of developing a vision itself.

One of the main reasons we set a vision, though, is because it makes the future visible to all the people in the company. So they can help us plan and get there.

The definition of visible is "Perceivable by the eye; capable of being seen. Apparent; observable; evident. At hand; available; manifest." We want the people in the company to have a visible future so that they know where they are going and how they can optimize their efforts to get there.

Vision answers the corporate question, "Where are we going?" It also must answer some of the question of "How are we going to get there?" Both of these questions must be answered firmly enough to provide visibility, but loosely enough so as not to stifle creativity.

> **The key objective of such a process is to create a filter for ideas.**

A good product development methodology evolves from the corporate vision and must provide a forum to resolve differences, define roles, eliminate unnecessary confusion and measure the effectiveness of the process itself. It should keep people from heading off on their own, but, at the same time, not stifle individual efforts. Most importantly, the new paradigm is that product development is a company-wide effort, requiring the participation of all the departments—not just Engineering. The key objective of such a process is to create a filter for ideas, reducing the huge number of potential new product ideas to a few products actually under development. We live in a world of limited resources—both money and engineering talent—and new product development is expensive. More expensive, in fact, than our balance sheet would indicate when we factor in sales training costs, collateral material, set-ups for our computers or factory equipment and other "hidden" expenses. Think of the process as a funnel. We want to spend very little money and resources for the multitude of potential ideas, concentrating our resources on those ideas that we feel certain will succeed.

So how do we craft a new product development process that follows this new vision?

Deserialization

For a start, we need to see an end of that serial process we discussed in the previous chapter. Before we go any further, we need to clear up some discrepancies with the serial concept. When people talk about the serial process, they're referring to the department-to-department hand-offs. One of the side-effects of these hand-offs is that each department develops their piece of the new product, then passes it on to the next department.

Engineering designs the product, then passes it to Manufacturing. Manufacturing designs the process to produce the product, then passes it to Marketing. Marketing designs the sales brochure and operating manual, and so on. The first thing we have to do to craft a new methodology is see the product *in toto*. A new product is not just the box itself or the new service. Instead, it's the sum of all the parts necessary to making that product a success. In addition to the product itself, the list includes operating manuals, sales brochures, sales staff training, customer service staff training, replacement parts, packaging, order entry mechanisms, delivery to the customer and any other critical piece of minutiae that surrounds a new product. If that new product is a service, and it's going to require a wholesale revision of our phone system, that revision must be considered as part of the new product development process.

Instead of handing off the new product from department to department for their contributions, we're going to be developing the product, the process, the order entry scheme, the brochures, the sales training, all the assorted collateral material at the same time, in parallel.

There's been a lot written about designing in parallel, mostly in reference to industry, where the product and the process to build that product are now being designed at the same time. The concept isn't so revolutionary once we refine our view of the new product to encompass all the elements of that product. Just like it wouldn't make sense to design every part of a bicycle except the wheels, then start on the wheels when we were finished with everything else, it doesn't make sense to design a service, then start designing the delivery system for the service when we are finished.

Creating a new product in parallel can substantially cut the time it takes to get a new product to market, and it can improve the

Product Development
New Paradigm: Parallel Paths

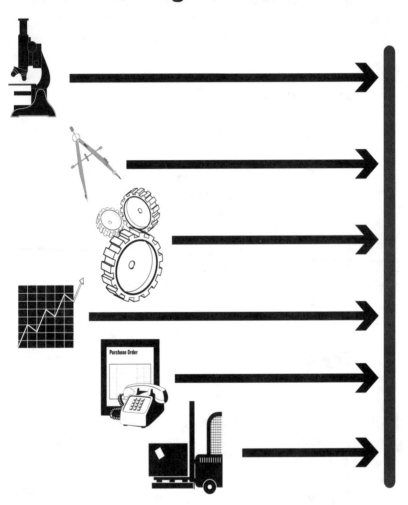

quality of both the process and the product. But only with a couple of caveats. To really speed up the development process, it's necessary to provide a framework for people to work together. Under the serial process, there's a vacuum in which there is no forum to resolve natural conflicts that will arise in the process. For the parallel process to work smoothly, we must define people's roles in the process. For example, for a football team to come out of the huddle and line up quickly, ready to play, each person has to know his or her position. Not everyone can be the quarterback or the receiver. We don't want to define our roles too tightly for fear of constricting creativity, but, by necessity, we must have roles. But, again with our football analogy, people must be able to adapt as the play develops.

> If a company just increases the track record to four out of 10, the result is an astounding 33 percent improvement in the effective output of new products.

Performing the development activities in parallel has another danger zone. If we have to restart the process in the middle, we'll waste more resources than would have been lost in the old serial approach. It stands to reason, then, that for the parallel process to avoid becoming a trap, we must provide a method to define the new product clearly enough in the beginning so that changes during the process will be minimized.

Batting Practice

We've also got to increase our batting average—more products to market in the same time frame.

To increase our output of effective new products, we could decide to increase product development expenditures from 10 to 11 percent of sales. The most often touted and discussed measure of a company's commitment to new product development. This would effectively increase the amount of product development activity by 10 percent. This is, however, the brute force (and expensive) way to increase the output.

A more effective way is to improve the "batting average" of new products, which can result in remarkable gains. Consider the company that develops three successful new products out of 10 attempts. If this company just increases the track record to four out of 10, the result is an astounding 33 percent improvement in the effective output of new products. The effect is the same as increasing the product development expenditures from 10 to 13.3 percent. The irony of the example is that most businesses today don't even enjoy a 3 out of 10 new product success rate, so the gains to be made are even larger.

With these types of gains to be made, it's strange that more companies are not strongly committed to increasing their "batting average." The old marketing and product development planning methods have literally worn people out, leaving them resigned to low success rates with new products. Its a shame that the "it's black magic" mentality has people buffaloed into not earnestly trying to improve product planning. The MAP process, though, can get us past the black magic stage and back into the ballpark.

New Tools

The way to make a company-wide parallel development process really hum is to know that we're developing the right product in the first place. However, we haven't had such great luck with accomplishing that in the past.

We've used lots of tools for studying the customers needs and wants—surveys, questionnaires, focus groups, gap analysis and many, many others.

These tools, while still valuable, are no longer sufficient in and of themselves. We need some new tools, tools that use all of the resources of the company to plan new products, without distracting people from their primary responsibilities. With fast-moving markets and scarce resources, we've got to improve our batting average in new product planning, and that means getting close, closer, closest to our customers.

That also means new tools to help us understand our customers and the problems that our products are solving. Products have to be useful to the customer. If the product is not useful and attractive, no amount of expertise in other functions will make it succeed. We have seen several companies build state of the art factories for a product that couldn't be given away. The result is always the same—failure. In fact, some recent research into consumer products seems to indicate that the presence of a feature the customer does not want negatively influences the customer's buying decision, even if the product's other features are to the customer's liking. In other words, we can no longer throw functions and features at our customers in the hope that we'll hit the right mix. (Does any of this argument sound familiar to you software developers out there?) Instead of the old shotgun, we've got to haul out the rifle and aim.

> It's not enough to simply ask a customer, "What do you want?"

The MAP Toolbox includes a whole series of aiming devices. Some of those, such as S-curve analysis, shows you how to better understand where your product is in its effective life cycle and how that relates to your customers. Which is important when you start allocating R&D money. Other tools show you how to get closer to your customers, then turn that knowledge into products.

Outside Helpers

The new methodology has to involve customers and other "outsiders" in the product development efforts.

People have recognized the need to understand the customers situation for a long time. As we've mentioned before, it's not enough to simply ask a customer, "What do you want?" But some of your customers can and will actually teach you their business so you can use their knowledge and expertise to determine how to best serve them. You can use their actual business environment to test the product during early phases of development. They'll help you to determine if the product can be easily installed serviced and used. They can be test readers for manuals. Often, they'll coach you on how their purchase decisions are made and what approval authority is for various organizational levels.

Many times, the "if we had only known" questions can and will be answered by the right customer. So early on, even during the replanning of the company's strategy and definitely during the detailed definition of a particular product, the customer should be involved. Under nondisclosure agreements, they can be given detailed definition of products to critique before the design of the product even begins.

You can also take prototypes to their service people and actually have them install the prototypes. In the process, they can give you valuable feedback on how to make the product easier or less expensive to install and service. They can tell you how easy your product is to include in their fabrication processes. Are they easy and convenient to handle? Is your material the right size? How much scrap results in their process? Are your preliminary data sheets difficult to understand or is there data missing?

Under MAP, the process is designed in parallel with the product.

Key suppliers also need to be involved in your product development processes from the beginning as well. There is a gold mine of knowledge, processes and technology that you may not have. If this knowledge and technology can give your products a competitive edge, it needs to be mined early in the product development process.

It is important to recognize that not all the processes and technology can or should be developed in the company itself. It is equally important to know how to decide which technology should be pursued internally and which to let others pursue for you. Sometimes it is prudent—no, necessary—to use the manufacturing processes of other enterprises.

In the past the "make-buy decision" was made mostly on the basis of cost-of-making verses price-of-buying.

Today, two other factors must be taken into account:

First, will the process, knowledge or technology involved differentiate us from the competition?

Second, are we committed to becoming or remaining the best in the world at that particular issue?

If the answer to these questions is yes, we will develop the knowledge, even if we are not the low-cost supplier at the time. If the answer to either question is no, we may want to discontinue the pursuit, even if we are currently practicing it cost effectively. You need to be the best at each facet of the business and should not dilute resources by using them on endeavors where you are not committed to excellence. Therefore, even if a key process or technology is outside the company, it needs to be considered during product development.

Note that not all suppliers will be key to your success, and there will still be products that you will put out to bid to keep cheap.

Do It Quickly

No matter what we do, our methodology has to be based on moving fast. With the markets moving quickly and the competitors coming out of the woodwork, products must be planned, designed and introduced quickly—much more quickly than we've ever done before. "More and more, advanced manufacturers are learning that the time required to develop a new product has more influence on its success than its costs," says Charles H. House of Hewlett Packard, writing in the *Harvard Business Review*. Much of our inability to respond quickly comes from our slow-motion silo organizational approach to business. Silo organizations have a tendency to become bureaucratic and are slow to react to change, largely because no one person sees the overall picture.

In our new product development methodologies, we tended to see our problems in terms of bad people—poor work ethic, poorly educated, minimum wage, doesn't-give-a-darn, Japan got all the good managers. In truth, our people have done exactly what we've charged them to do. They've been victims of an outmoded, calcified process. "Once," says the *Harvard Business Review*, "time was money. Now it is more valuable than money."

In addition to moving from serial to parallel development, there are some other basic guidelines to speed to up the development machine:
   • Get good decision making widespread in the company
   • Remove non-value adding activities

• Increase people's productivity

Decisions must be made quickly, but they still must be made well. When people are waiting for a decision, time and critical resources are lost. However, people must be well informed and proficient in problem-solving skills to make good decisions. The challenge—and this is a major challenge—is to establish an organization that prepares and encourages all people to make good decisions. If the decision does require the involvement of others, people need to know how to quickly get the forum established to resolve the situation.

Removing non-value adding activities can be more difficult than is seems. We have developed products for so long with the existing methods that it is difficult for us to objectively tell what is value-adding and what is resource-wasting. However, by using the MAP process template and critically reviewing our processes, we can determine what can be discontinued without discarding the essential.

Process And Product

In the MIT study on American competitiveness, Made In America, it was found that American companies spend about two-thirds of their development resources on the development of the product and one-third on developing the process. Comparatively, Japanese companies spend the reverse, about one-third developing the product and two-thirds developing the process. We might assume that in the last ten years, with the tremendous focus on things Japanese—especially their new product development—that American companies might be changing their ways. On the contrary, the same study showed that the proportions have remained basically the same in the time period from 1976-1985, the last year that data is available.

We need to apply a more balanced amount of resources on the development of processes. Accommodations in the product and process during the design make the product more producible, and the processes more controllable.

Consider a product made of two pieces welded together. In

Resource Allocation
during development

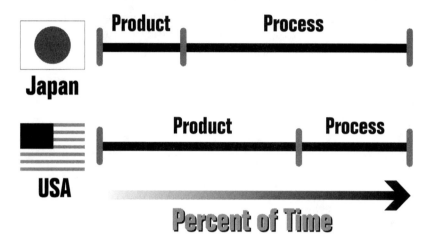

Japan — Product | Process

USA — Product | Process

Percent of Time

the past, designers prototyped the welding process in a engineering laboratory or, worse yet, subcontracted it to a local job shop. When the product was released to production, the welding design was based on the prototyping efforts.

After production release, Manufacturing began to build the product on actual production machinery. As they tried to weld the parts, they would begin to learn about the real process. Sometimes the material would be a problem, other times warpage because of the heating and cooling would be a problem. These problems weren't discovered earlier because the engineering lab equipment was different than the production equipment. Or, perhaps the process worked in the laboratory test-tubes, but failed when we tried to move it on-line. In the real world, the specifics are always different, and time and time again shipment of new products are delayed as the manufacturing process is ironed out.

Under MAP, the process is designed in parallel with the product. The prototypes are built on the production equipment under actual shop floor conditions. The process issues are ironed out at the same time that the product issues are ironed out.

The result of doing the product design and process design at the same time is fewer delays and change orders after production release. An additional bonus is that the actual cycle time to deliver quantity product to the customer is actually faster. Also, the accumulated knowledge and experience of the manufacturing people is brought to bear to design the quality and productivity into the product. The design is done right the first time, rather than redesigned by a series of change orders latter.

The New Vision

This, then is the vision we're going to be moving toward with the MAP process. The key concepts to remember are:
- Company-wide
- Fast
- Parallel
- Involving outsiders
- Process and product together

All these key concepts will figure in when we move into the MAP process itself. In the following section, we're going to be exploring the five phases and gates that make up the heart of the MAP process. The phases are:

1) Identifying customer Needs.
2) Establishing project Feasibility.
3) Defining the product.
4) Designing the product.
5) The Launch.

As we examine each step, remember to avoid the confusion with the serial process. The serial process refers to the old paradigm of department-to-department hand-offs. Our new paradigm, the MAP process, addresses our key concepts and involves every department at each phase.

Chapter 4

Phases And Gates

All product development efforts go through a series of steps, which involve decision points at each step. Eastman Kodak coined the phrase and named the document describing their development process "Phases and Gates." Their terminology has been adopted by many companies and moved into widespread use. We're using it here because it provides a convenient shorthand for dealing with the new product development process.

"Phases" represent the steps of the development process. During each phase, certain deliverables—that is, specific items such as detailed plans, estimates, prototypes, the product itself, anything that must be delivered before the product passes into another phase—are produced. We have found through painful trial-and-error that five phases is optimum for the process to work efficiently. I have seen development methodologies that define as many as 22 phases. They are every bit as slow as the old serial process. I have also seen new product development methodologies with fewer than five phases, with unfortunate side effects such as poor product definition. Five is the optimum balance between speed and control.

Remember, the five phases of the MAP process are:
1) Needs

2) Feasibility

3) Defining

4) Designing

5) Launch

There's going to be a tendency, however, to add more and more phases under the guise of better and better control. Instead of better control, the process will be stifled and begin to grind to a halt. "If it's not carefully managed," says one of the Eastman Kodak's new product development managers, "the whole concept of phases and gates can become a real impediment in getting a product to market."

MAP Process
Phases & Gates

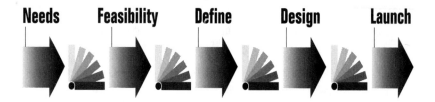

These five phases are separated by "gates." The "gates" are the review and decision points in-between the phases. At the gates, the deliverables are measured and evaluated in a specified review process. There are three possible decisions at these gate points: Proceed as planned, modify the plan, or stop the development effort.

Gates allow us to cut through the chaos and confusion that result from an imbalance between resources and ideas—too many ideas; too few resources. In fact, the gates allow us to maximize the throughput of ideas by effective management of those resources.

The gates also provide specific points where we must make the "hold 'em/fold 'em" decision. In the old paradigm, it was a haphazard, informal decision. Sometimes that decision was never made. But the gates force us to consider the go/no go decision and evaluate whether we want to continue funding the project.

The five phases are each described in detail in their own chapters, but a brief overview is helpful to understand the whole process. Think of the five phases as a funnel. At the widest point of the funnel, the first phase, we're trying to collect as many ideas as we can. As we move down through the funnel, fewer and fewer ideas get through the winnowing process. As those ideas move into development and actual projects, ideally, only the best will make it through the narrowest point of the funnel—Launch. Remember, we're funneling resources as well, spending a small amount on each idea at the top of the funnel and increasingly larger amounts as the project moves toward a successful launch.

> The gates also provide specific points where we must make the "hold 'em/fold 'em" decision.

In the Needs Phase, our focus is on trying to understand the customer's needs in enough detail that we can put ourselves in the customer's shoes. During this process we maintain a "needs list," which is basically a list of what our customers need. Marketing manages the "needs list," but anyone can get an idea placed on the list. At this point, there's no limit to the number of needs we have—there shouldn't be a limit, because there's no limit on understanding the marketplace.

Feasibility is a very short, often four-week or less, phase that, for the first time, includes all the functions of the company to see if there's any obvious reason for not continuing to pursue the idea. Feasibility begins the transition from need to product. It allows us to get more information on the risks involved and the possibilities of success without the commitment of large funds.

Typically, the Definition Phase, where we finish the transition from need to product idea, is our weak point. In this phase, we create a detailed plan for the product and the process to minimize changes that might occur during the design phase. This phase is also where we stand to make our biggest gains. An excellent definition leads to a painless design.

The Design Phase where the detail definition is converted into the information required for the company to sell, order, produce and service the product.

Finally, at the Launch Phase of the product, the product is offered for sale. The sales training efforts and customer training efforts are carried out. Then, we get our report card to see how well we've done.

The Gatekeepers

Who monitors the gates at each different phase?

Every company has some person or group that addresses the new product planning and coordination challenges. These people are, in effect, the gatekeepers. The term gatekeeper arises because the most effective time to plan and give direction to the new product efforts is at the gates before and in between the various phases of new product development. In some companies, especially smaller companies, the gatekeeping function is very informal: in others, it is very formal. In the MAP process, we have very formal gatekeepers who are, in effect, the keepers of the new product development methodology. It's a tough job, and not for the weak of heart.

Let's begin, as it were, at the starting gate.

When the company is small, a single person—usually the founder/entrepreneur—determines where resources will be used and what products will be developed. Often, the process is informal, and decisions are made by "gut feel." If the decisions are good and the enterprise grows, and the process becomes more involved. The number of decisions increase, and communication becomes more of an issue as more and more people become involved. Either formally or informally, a certain set of people becomes the core of the new product planning process. This collection of people act as the primary gatekeepers for the product development process.

In the MAP process, the gatekeepers are formally organized as the Product Development Review Board (PDRB). This group has the responsibility for allocating resources based on the information presented to it by development teams and representatives of the company departments. The PDRB makes the go/no-go/change decisions at each of the gates, except for the final gate. At that gate, the product development team itself makes the decision to release the new product to production.

The PDRB serves as the "bridge" between the company's overall strategy and it's new product planning. The PDRB executes the company's strategy and tactics through the selection of marketplace needs that will go on to be defined, designed and launched. The MAP process is, literally, the map that allows us to move from corporate strategic plans to which specific new products we must develop to support those plans.

When it's necessary to change the company's strategy or tactics, it's the PDRB that presents the situation to the Board of Directors and brings about the necessary modifications.

The meetings of the PDRB provide a forum to bring new product development issues to the forefront. Some of those issues include reviewing any project in any phase, discussing new market data, selecting the next project as resources become available, making the go/no-go decision at a gate, reviewing the performance of the overall process by discussing quality measurements or disseminating technology, process and marketplace information.

The resource allocation function is critical—this is not the place for the "squeaky wheel" to get the grease.

Putting It All On Paper

A published product development policy is a critical component of the MAP process, and the PDRB is the device for making that policy a reality. Here are some of the issues that need to be addressed in an ideal MAP policy:
- Quality considerations before product release.
- Drivers for new products.

• Who is involved in new product development.

• How are market, technical and manufacturing risks to be managed.

• Measurable objectives for new product development.

• How many ideas will be pursued.

• Total capacity.

• Length of time for Definition and Design phases.

• Financial thresholds for PDRB approval.

• Members of the PDRB and their roles.

• Frequency and schedule of PDRB meetings.

Here are some of the possible answers to those questions (A complete sample MAP policy is included in the index):

1) New products will be defect-free. If the products are not in a defect-free state, they will not be released to production. We define a defect as a failure to comply or perform with product requirements, which must be stated in users' terms—that is, no technological gobbledygook. A desired enhancement, on the other hand, is not a defect. If we held up every product for enhancements, which can be defined as a change in the user requirements, we would never get the product to market. The business magazines and newspapers are full of "tried to do everything for everybody and ended up doing very little for anybody" stories.

2) Products will be developed that fulfill actual customer needs. When a product is developed for a "want" that is not an actual need, the relationships between the customers and the company are compromised. Our customers buy our products based on the trust that the products will provide true value.

3) Product development is a company-wide effort involving all areas. Manufacturing, Sales, Marketing, Product Service, Quality Assurance, Finance and Engineering must be involved from the very beginning, especially during the Definition Phase. The quality, manufacturability, serviceability and other desired attributes are to be designed into the product as the product itself is designed.

4) The technical risk of new products is managed by Engineering. Engineering must be sure that the company has, or can

acquire, the product technology to develop the proposed product. New product planning is still a group effort, and while all the product technology-related activities may not be done in Engineering, Engineering is considered the facilitator when it comes to managing the product technology.

Risk management isn't an easy task. Some risk will have to be taken in most worthwhile new product efforts. So Engineering will have to set "stretch goals," but those goals must be manageable. The worst thing that can happen in new product development is spending 150 percent of the estimated resources and then realize you can never get the product to market.

> Some risk will have to be taken in most worthwhile new product efforts.

The market risk is managed by Marketing. Even when a new product is created exactly as defined, the customers may not purchase it. Marketing has to facilitate the understanding of the customers' situation and the presentation of the products, so that new products correctly address the customers' needs—and the customers understand the value of a product. The days of building a better mousetrap and having the world beat a path to your door are over. Steven Jobs did indeed build a better mousetrap with his NeXT computer. Remember the NeXT computer?

Process risk is managed by Manufacturing. The processes required to manufacture and deliver the products to the customers need to be defined, designed and implemented at the same time as the product, and Manufacturing coordinates that linkage.

5) There must be a measurable objective for new product revenues. What a shock! How do we know whether we are successful unless we have realistic, measurable goals? But you must have an objective. There needs to be enough effort spent on new products that the product lines are current. The latest proven technology must be used to fill the customers needs in the most reliable cost-effective manner. The other end of the spectrum is that you can not churn the products so rapidly the sales people and customers never have time to master their application.

6) New products will only be started when the required resources are available. Resources can become available by completion of a previous project, new resources being added to the company, or the cancellation by the PDRD of an existing project. The total amount of product development resources in each department is planned during the annual budget and financial planning process. Each department is then expected to manage to their budget. There needs to be a statement of how the utilization of the resources are managed and how the amount of resources available is managed.

> It takes a strong person to make sure the process is being followed; that there are no short cuts in the process.

7) We need to set a target length for each phase of the MAP process. My company, for example, has a one-month time limit for Feasibility, a six-month time limit for Definition and a 12-month-or-less limit for Design. Needs and Launch are both on-going phases.

8) All development efforts that exceed a certain level—we use $20,000—in expenditures require PDRB approval. Projects that require less than $20,000 can be authorized by a department head. (This is to prevent the stifling effect of requiring even small efforts to be approved by PDRB.)

In the MAP process, the PDRB meets every four weeks, with the meetings scheduled a year in advance. All members of the PDRB are required to schedule their activities so that they can attend every meeting, because the new product planning activities are too important to be delegated "down the line."

The members of the PDRB are the President, Vice President of Sales, Manager of Marketing, Vice President of Finance, Vice President of Manufacturing, the head of New Product Development, and the Engineering Manager. As various projects are reviewed, many of the team members from the various projects are in attendance to present information and answer questions. (For a complete breakdown of PRDB members and roles, see the Appendix.)

My job title demonstrates the new MAP paradigm. I'm Vice

President of Manufacturing and Product Development. The title was created when we still thought that product development and engineering were nearly synonymous. However, as time passed and we evolved the MAP process, the meaning of the title significantly changed. I'm still responsible for Manufacturing and Engineering, but the Product Development part of the title now means something very different. As product development has become a company-wide effort, my responsibilities have shifted to coordinating the product development methodology rather than running a product development department.

Each department has an equal opportunity to influence the development of a product. The departments balance each other and the marketing-driven, technology-driven, or process-driven extremes are avoided.

The Process Facilitator

In addition to the PDRB, there needs to be an individual who facilitates the MAP process. It takes a strong person to make sure the process is being followed; that there are no short cuts in the new product development process. There will be strong pressures to cut the work short and fill in the details later, especially during Definition. Then there's the inevitable temptation when your best customer calls with the BFO, Big Fantastic Order, to throw process out the window. Forget resource allocation! Forget risks! Let's be responsive to that customer (and BFO). We have a technical phrase for the fire drill that results from constant BFO lust—chaos.

And making sure that, say, Definition is complete is far different from having an opinion on what the definition of a product is. From our own experiences, we've found that the gatekeeper (or group that functions as gatekeeper) needs to be able to explain the necessities of each phase to others in the company who might not be part of or understand the new product development process "loop" and, consequently, may be applying some of the pressure. To prepare for that eventuality, remember these four points:

1) Be prepared to logically explain the ramifications of failing to complete any phase. Have past examples that everyone is familiar with to reinforce the reality of waste and redo that occurs with we short-cut the process. Avoid pointing fingers or the dread "I told you so," but reinforce that the MAP process is the best way to avoid the same problems all over again.

2) If more powerful forces demand that, say, the project be started without a complete Definition, state your case, then roll up your sleeves to make the project a success despite the absence of a complete definition. Hopefully, you've gotten far enough along in the definition process to head off the worst of the problems.

3) Develop your own tools to make the phases easier and better understood.

4) Put a program in place to improve people's communications skills. Lack of communication is the biggest problem with new product development, and it can frustrate people to the point that they just want to get back to the old, informal "just do it" system.

Chapter 5

Phase One: Customer Needs

Phase One in the product development process is to understand the customer's needs, then gather the product and business knowledge to most effectively fulfill those needs.

A market for a new product can be created by any of a number of factors. It may, for example, be based on technological change. Pocket calculators could not practically exist until integrated circuit technology progressed to a certain point. Sometimes opportunity is driven by changes in style or fashion, particularly true in the clothing and jewelry business. This year's short and tight is next year's long and baggy. Changes in social trends, laws or regulations can affect what will sell and what will not.

Frequently, the agent of change is the continual learning process of the customer and the changing aspirations that result from that learning process. Solving existing problems puts new problems at the top of the list, and the new problems and desires result in new market opportunities.

Usually, a combination of factors contribute to the need, or demand, for new products. Look at the personal computer industry. Many factors—evolving technology, marketplace trends and customer expectations, to name just a few—are constantly ebbing and flowing through the personal computer industry. Computer product life cycles are shrinking, graying the hair of new product developers. In the small computer industry, observed *The Wall Street Journal* recently, product life cycles are "brutish and short."

> In the small computer industry, observed *The Wall Street Journal* recently, product life cycles are "brutish and short."

Granted, determining which ideas will be successful and which features and functions should be incorporated into a new product ranks as one of the toughest jobs in industry. But new product developers can be successful, even in these turbulent times, by following three rules of new product planning:

1) Understand—in depth—not only the customer's wants, but the customer's true needs.

2) Understand the methods and technologies available for meeting those needs.

3) Use knowledge of technology and business processes to define new products that will best fulfill the needs.

Understanding The Customer's Needs

The closer you are to your customers, the more you'll be able to understand their problems and needs. The better you understand your customers' business situation and the way they make decisions, the more likely you are to succeed. We accept, as Tom Peters writes, that we must stay close to our customers. But which customers, and how do we stay close to them? In the past, we've gone to great lengths to figure out what our customers' wants and needs are and, at times, we've done very well. The concept of "market research" is aimed at the question, "What do they want?"—often resulting in multiple choice answers! The problem is that many times, when asked, an individual doesn't actually know what he or she really needs. And, when the moment of truth comes—time to sign the check—the customer may decide our products and services don't satisfy the true needs.

This is especially true in breakthrough products—the home run. For example, who would have predicted a ground swell demand for automatic bread-making machines in the months before they were introduced? Our traditional efforts in market research have grown more sophisticated over the years, and they include user groups, focus groups, customer surveys, informal assessments, guesses by "knowledgeable people," and following big purchase orders. These techniques have validity, but new tools and perspectives are also required.

User groups and focus groups are exactly what the names imply. They may be independent groups, such as blossomed in the early days of personal computers, or they may be groups sponsored by the manufacturer and/or provider. A major strength of these groups is that they are usually heavily populated with customers, or potential customers. User group and focus group approaches also provide a valuable forum for brainstorming. Any time you have a group of people together discussing an issue, the brainstorming affect may lead to creative leaps unlikely to occur with an individual contemplating the situation.

People's thought processes have been paralyzed by the existing paradigm.

It is important, as in any brainstorming session, not to let the naturally dominant players overwhelm the process. It's equally important not to try to agree on the approach that will be taken, a counter-productive move that may stifle creativity. What you are interested in is your customers discussing their business problems in an open manner that may lead to good new product ideas.

Many of the marketing techniques rely on the approach of asking the customer, "What do you want?" There is an inherent drawback to obtaining marketing information this way. Often, when we ask the question, people are not prepared to answer; they have not thought out the situation, or their thought processes have been paralyzed by the existing paradigm.

Exacerbating this paralysis of the thought processes is the survey that asks "what do you want?" and then provides multiple choice answers. This situation is further aggravated by people's desire to "help;" i.e., the "what do you want?" technique has the potential of putting the person on the spot, but people generally want to be helpful and will answer the question—whether they've given the matter a lot of thought or not.

This isn't a critical situation if you're asking directions to a fast-food establishment. But suppose you're trying to decide how to spend a significant portion of your product development resources. If you ask for an opinion, you're going to get just that—an opinion. The less the customer has thought about it, the more likely the opinion will resemble what he already has thought about. "When you've got a hammer," goes the old saying, "everything looks like a nail."

There's Always An Answer

Another major danger of the "what do you want?" question is that you may prematurely predispose a potential customer with a specific new product definition, and it may not be the one you are going to pursue. Even if they haven't adequately analyzed the situation, they feel obligated to answer the question. As they answer, they begin to develop a vested interest in their off-the-cuff answers. The stage is set for, "You don't listen to me. I told you exactly what I wanted, and you didn't do it."

The survey approach has its place. However, the survey is, in my opinion, the least effective and potentially the most dangerous way to gather real world information from customers. Responses to the survey may actually fool you into thinking you understand the situation, when in fact you don't.

What else can we use besides these established, but flawed, techniques? The "what else" is simple to state and difficult to do. The what else is to learn our customer's business well enough that we can put ourselves in his or her shoes. When we understand our customer's business, we are in a better position to estimate which of the many wants and needs will be of high enough value to result in purchases. The key to mastering this technique is to spend initial—and continual—efforts learning their business, instead of just selling existing products or trying to get their endorsement of our new product ideas.

For example, if we are manufacturers of industrial instrumentation, we need to learn how the Clean Air Act is going to affect our customers, how it will change their purchase decisions. It is important not to confuse the selling process with marketing research. As soon as we start on the sale of our existing or new products, the learning process gets pushed to the background. Or, worse yet, we actually stop the learning process as we start the selling process. If you build a relationship with the customer that encourages them to discuss their situation, even if you think it may not relate directly to your products, you can learn:

> When we understand our customer's business, we are in a better position to estimate which of the many wants and needs will be of high value.

• What they think most positively affects their career or social standing

• What causes them the most embarrassment or pain

• The issue(s) they believe most important to their bosses or social peers

• Whether they use their time productively or unproductively

These and similar issues integrate to determine the next purchase of goods or services. An astute individual's experiences and observations are more reliable than an off-the-cuff answer to "What do you want?" As you and the customer review the situation, you'll experience a broad-based learning process. Ideally, you'll develop a feel for the priority of the potential products—what the customer will buy now and what will be postponed until next year.

A Company-wide Effort

Making marketing a company-wide effort improves the understanding of the customer's actual situation. Instead of marketing being done solely by the people in the Marketing Department, we enlist the support of sales, service, engineering and other functions. Every time someone calls on the customer, attends a trade show or participates in a business conference, we can determine more about needs and problems.

This information is not collected by asking the outmoded standby question, "What do you want?" Rather, we try to determine what the customer actually needs by observing the customer's actions, reviewing the customer's actual experiences and determining what product-related decisions have been made previously.

Marketing is the prime facilitator—the driver—of the needs phase, and Marketing's main role is to manage the marketing risk of new product development. During new product planning, this risk is managed in two decision-making processes: the selection of needs to pursue and the selection of product ideas to fulfill the need.

Most current approaches to the selection of a new product focus on ideas first. We collect ideas, then try to discuss the relative merits of each idea despite an inadequate understanding of the potential customer's actual situation. The order needs to be reversed. We must first adequately and completely understand the customer's situation, then focus on product ideas. When Marketing pieces together the information gathered by everyone into an accurate picture of the marketplace, the stage is set for successful selection and definition of new products.

Everyone needs to participate in gathering information. When sales people make their calls, they should note any new information about the customers. To be sure, we need to avoid turning our sales people into full-time marketers. Their primary function is still to make the sale and service the account. But if we use the sales techniques taught by companies such as Wilson Learning and Miller Heiman, with relatively minor modifications, the sales and marketing information-gathering become synergistic, and each area will grow stronger.

For example Wilson Learning offers a course— "The Versatile Salesperson" —that familiarizes people with the different social styles of individuals. The course teaches how to recognize the different styles, what their strengths and weaknesses are, and how to relate effectively to each style. A person armed with this knowledge can establish an effective relationship with a large variety of customers.

Miller Heiman teaches courses like strategic selling. Strategic selling familiarizes people with the concepts necessary to analyze accounts, determine the different buying influences and get customers to help you understand their situation.

Not only the sales people can support Marketing's role. As engineers contact customers, they should try to determine the tools and technologies the customers are already using. This information can be used to make new product plans compatible with the customers' existing investments. Engineers and other employees can also use field experience to help paint the picture of what is most important to potential customers. As field service people work at customer sites, they can document the customer's preferred method of servicing products and the customer's expectations in terms of response times, spare parts, etc.

> Marketing's main role is to manage the marketing risk of new product development.

You get close to the customer by learning about the potential customer's situation. You need to understand the most pressing problems the customer is facing and what is causing the customer the most *pain*. It's likely that future resources will be spent on these sensitive areas and that opportunities exist to help the customer with a new product or service. It is equally important to know when the sensitive areas are not related to our business, so we can accurately assess the customer's probability of purchasing our new products.

In his book, *Managing Innovation*, John S. Rydz discusses

how one company, Diebold, stayed close enough to its customers to understand their needs. Diebold, a maker of safes and vaults, had a president, Ray Koontz, who was dedicated to providing the equipment to fulfill needs in the banking and finance industry.

During the 1960s, the banking industry was undergoing a profound change from centralized banks to banks consisting of many branch offices. The banking laws were being liberalized to include the branch bank concept, and this change was causing significant modifications in the operations of the banks and financial institutions. The number of transactions were increasing as the branch banks provided the public with easier and more convenient access. At the same time, the security challenges were different. Instead of having to protect only a few large banks, many smaller and geographically dispersed branches now required adequate protection. While many companies fail to understand and adjust to fundamental changes in the market place, Diebold was able to adapt its business to the changing business of its customers. Ray Koontz had built a company culture of staying close to the customer, understanding their situation and then meeting their needs.

If Diebold had focused only on the technology and what technology made possible, it is doubtful the company would have successfully made the necessary transitions. The emerging technologies in this industry could provide an endless variety of fascinating options. Everyone on the Diebold team was encouraged to focus on and help understand the customer's needs. Marketing and sales people paid strict attention to state banking laws.

Everyone was encouraged to participate in conferences, seminars and forums where security trends and their impact on banking were analyzed. Diebold managers met with key bankers. All experiments conducted in banks using either Diebold's or the competition's equipment were closely monitored. R&D people toured banks to familiarize themselves with banking operational requirements. In Washington D.C., the people who serviced and sold Diebold equipment to the intelligence networks kept the company informed about potential banking regulations.

The people in the company stayed in touch with the American Bankers Association to learn about the challenges within the industry. Harry Parr, Diebold's financial vice president, strengthened his network through his banking contacts. Close contacts were established with the Federal Bureau of Investigation and other government security agencies to analyze events involving security and Diebold's type of equipment.

In summary, Raymond Koontz had everyone involved in understanding the customer's business so Diebold could predict the needs. This allowed Diebold to leap-frog the competition and lead the industry. Frequently, Diebold knew what its customers needed before the customers themselves. Diebold was able to determine that steel vaults would need to be augmented with electronic alarm systems to adequately protect the many branches of the new banking system; that ATMs (automatic teller machines) would be needed to help with the increased volume of transactions demanded by the banks' changing customer base, and that telephone line security systems would be required to confidentially handle the increasing volumes of information going through the branch banking environment.

> If you learn the market place thoroughly enough, you will be able to successfully predict which problems customers will pay to have solved.

During the information gathering process, we try to discover any changing business situations that are likely to affect what is important to the customer and, therefore, what the customer is likely to purchase in the future. When new legislation or regulations are enacted, it is essential to know which rulings will affect the customer and what the effect might be. In the petrochemical and power generation industries, for example, it was important to recognize the potential impact of the Clean Air Act. The new laws and accompanying regulations were going to change what was important and how and where money and resources were going to be spent. If you learn the market place thoroughly enough to put yourself in the customer's shoes at purchase time, you will be able to successfully predict which new products will succeed—which problems customers will pay to have solved.

Product Technology And Business Processes

We need more than just an understanding of the marketplace to succeed, however. We also need the technology and the business processes to bring our solutions to the customers' problems to reality. Like understanding the marketplace, learning product technology and business processes is a perpetual task.

Every day a newer, better, bigger, faster technology is announced. Higher temperature plastic, stronger fabric, faster electronic components, less expensive information systems and on and on. These advances provide opportunities to create reliable, low-cost products with more features and functions—if we're able to access the technology.

> Learning product technology and business processes is a perpetual task.

The most successful competitors not only fulfill the need, they use premiere technology and business processes to do so. The most successful competitors learn the best way to fulfill needs even if it is not necessarily the area in which they excel.

A particular need usually can be fulfilled in several ways. An insurance company's need for an information system could be satisfied with the purchase of a computer and software. On the other hand, the need may be fulfilled by a time-sharing service for which the customer does not have to buy and maintain hardware and software. The best solution is the one that provides the most value to the customer.

Keeping the product development cycle short requires that product technology be learned in parallel—i.e., concurrently—with the market research. If research is required to locate and learn technology and processes after the need is identified, the development of a product is delayed. The more knowledge already available, the shorter the total development cycle. While Marketing pieces together the marketplace, the design people stay abreast of the technology that can be used to develop products.

Manufacturing, product service, customer service and all other departments must also keep current with business practices that most effectively provide customers with answers to their needs. This also is an ongoing process done in parallel with market research. If there is a highly developed way to process customer orders accurately and quickly, new products must be defined so as to take advantage of the process. If an innovative process exists that can inexpensively and quickly service products, it must be considered when a new product approach is chosen.

The Needs Phase is unique among the product development phases because it is a continuous learning journey. During the process, the company's strategy and tactics are constantly reviewed, reinforced and/or modified. Based on the knowledge gained, the company's plans are fine-tuned to best fit the current understanding of the customer's needs and the changes in technology and business practices.

Ideally, we'd like to be one product development cycle ahead of our competition. A development cycle is defined as the time it takes a project to pass through the needs gate to the launch phase.

The Gate

At the needs gate, we are balancing "like to do" with "can do" by not letting items on the needs list pass through the gate until resources are available. It is the availability of resources that triggers the movement of ideas from the Needs Phase into the Feasibility Phase. As resources are freed up from other development efforts, or the company can access new resources, the opportunity opens up to start another development project. At that time, the PDRB selects the next market place need to go into the feasibility process.

The available resources also impacts the type of need that can be pursued in the near term. If a specific software resource is available, then needs that can be fulfilled with that particular software should be pursued. In the long-term, it is the responsibility of the department managers to ensure that the company's resources have the capability to develop products that satisfy marketplace requirements. In the Diebold case, it was the responsibility of management to ensure that electrical engineers were added to the metallurgical and mechanical engineering staff as the marketplace shifted from massive vaults to electronic alarms and secure electronic information transfer. In the short-term, it would be a waste of resources to try to build electronic alarm systems with metallurgical engineers.

> Ideally, we'd like to be one product development cycle ahead of our competition.

This gate is a snapshot in time of the continuous information gathering process and marks the transition between marketplace needs and new product definition.

Chapter 6

Phase Two: Feasibility

After we've assessed our customers' needs, the project moves to the Feasibility Phase. The main purpose of this phase is to determine quickly if there are any problems that could, perhaps should, kill the project. Accordingly, feasibility is first focused on risk management—if there's an obvious flaw that will prevent success, it's better to discover that flaw before time and other resources are spent defining the product in detail.

During the Needs Phase, all of the company's departments are involved in the collection of information, with Marketing conducting most of the study and analysis. The Feasibility Phase provides the first forum for a multi-functional review of the issues.

The Engineering department reviews the product technology ramifications: do we have the technology to build a product that will satisfy the need? Do we have the engineering resources to develop this product? Notice that this phase translates to the service sector as well—if the product is a service, the same questions apply. We might outline alternatives for producing the new product in this phase—staff up or contract out, for example—but the final decisions won't be made until the Definition Phase.

Sales must evaluate the effectiveness of the sales channels for the new product in the marketplace. Do our sales people reach the customers who have the need our product is filling? Is the sales force knowledgeable about the technology involved, on both the customer's and the company's ends? Can a training program be designed to bridge whatever gaps exist? For example, maybe our previous product or service required individual sales calls with many follow-ups to "land" the big order. The new product we're considering is very inexpensive. That requires us to reevaluate our sales channels to market the product without intensive sales calls. This is an issue that seems extremely reasonable, almost simplistic, yet pause for a moment to reflect on the personal computer market. Upon the birth of that market, some of the biggest players marketed inexpensive PCs the same way they had been marketing expensive mainframes. They lost.

> Manufacturing needs to evaluate the relationship between the proposed product and the existing manufacturing processes.

Manufacturing needs to evaluate the relationship between the proposed product and the existing manufacturing processes. If the new product requires sheet metal fabrication, do we have those facilities, or must we add them or contract them out? If the new product requires quick medical screening, is our existing diagnostic equipment able to meet the increased demand, or do we need to add diagnostic equipment or arrange to subcontract some of the work? Are our current manufacturing people capable of managing the new technologies involved in the product, or will extensive training and recruiting be involved?

In addition to the obvious benefits of having the different disciplines review the product idea from all angles, the brainstorming that occurs often can provide fresh, new perspectives and information about the potential risks and opportunities.

The Four Questions

The Feasibility Phase boils down to four questions:

1) Do we have the technology required to develop the new product?

2) Can we manufacture the product after it is developed?

3) Do our existing sales channels effectively address the customers who have the need?

4) Can we make money from the new product?

A negative answer to any one of the four questions doesn't necessarily shut the project down. It may be time for the company to reevaluate its capabilities and make changes to adapt to the marketplace. The classic example is Diebold, which once manufactured safes to protect money in banks, but now makes sophisticated electronic alarms systems and ATMs.

When there are negative answers to any one of the four questions, however, the decision to continue is never made lightly. A decision with such far-reaching consequences requires a major commitment from the company, with the complete understanding of what is happening. What needs to happen to make the new product feasible is often a change in the structure of the company. The worst-case scenario is to get half-way through the change and decide it's not worthwhile to continue. One of the most powerful aspects of the Feasibility Phase is bringing such issues out into the light at an early stage.

Consider an example of a company in the business of making cabinets for kitchens and bathrooms. The "needs" people discover an increasing demand for a new type cabinet with the sink integrated into the countertop. During the Feasibility Phase, one of the alternative architectures proposed calls for the fabrication of synthetic marble. The company's current fabrication facilities are comprised almost entirely of woodworking equipment, since the current process involves buying a sink from a subcontractor and dropping it into a hole in the countertop. But the trend in the marketplace can't be ignored, because it has the potential to affect a significant amount of future business. The investment in new equipment and training would be high, and there's no guarantee that the marketplace is going to wholeheartedly embrace synthetic marble. The decision? Proceed into the Definition Phase, but subcontract the early production of the synthetic marble.

The Feasibility Phase is fixed-length and corresponds to the time between PDRB meetings. The four weeks between meetings is sufficient time to uncover any obvious reasons that a project should not go forward, or to reach agreement on the tactics to be used for tough situations.

During this four weeks, the first steps are also taken to define the product or service. Alternative architectures are evaluated, as are existing business practices and processes. The final decisions will be made in the Definition Phase.

Transitions

The transition from need to product can be fraught with perils. To be successful, the issues of need and product must be tightly yoked together, but—at the same time—we must remain aware that they are two separate issues. Take the specialty drill bit manufacturer, whose product consisted of bits for drilling small holes in very hard materials. The company thought in terms of increasingly exotic metals to survive the high temperatures of drilling ceramic-like materials. One day, though, the company discovered that sales had dropped dramatically. It seems the need was not for drill bits, but for holes—the company had been obsoleted by new laser technology.

> To be successful, the issues of need and product must be tightly yoked together.

Now look at a second company, founded as an environmental consulting group whose initial products were water studies, environmental impact assessments and the like. Unlike the drill company's management, however, the directors of the environmental company realized their marketplace didn't actually need reports, studies and more piles of paper. What their customers needed were permits that would allow them to remain in business, and more economical and effective remediation efforts. Based on their assessment, the environmental consultants shifted their product from "reports" to "solutions." The company's success is a direct result of a clear understanding of the difference between needs and the products that fulfill those needs.

The Gate

At the end of the Feasibility Phase, the information and evaluations collected on both the need and the product is presented to the PDRB. This presentation serves two purposes:

The first is to enable the PDRB to make the critical go/no-go decision on the project. The second purpose is to provide the PDRB with more detail on the need and the new product itself, which helps keep issues focused as the new product development process continues.

If the team's recommendation is to continue the project, a due date for the detailed definition is established. The date is recorded and used to make both project and process measurements. The date the Definition Phase begins is also recorded, so that the elapsed time for the Definition Phase can be measured and tracked. If the PDRB agreed with the "go" recommendation, the project passes through the feasibility gate and enters the Definition Phase.

Chapter 7

Phase Three: Definition

This is a "Big Fat Claim," but it has certainly held true in our experience: the biggest gains in efficiency will come from improving the definition of the new product. In our zeal to get started with a new product concept, we often don't take the time to define what we are doing in enough detail to see the potential consequences—often subtle—of our concept. Without a comprehensive, detailed definition, the executors of the product often do not understand the requirements, so instead do what they think should be done based on their interpretation of the inadequate definition. Under these circumstances, executors is perhaps an appropriate word.

In the MAP process, the ideas that pass through the gate at the end of the Feasibility Phase are defined in detail before the design of the product begins. Many a product has been launched on the basis of a one liner; i.e., an optimistic but vague sentence beginning with words like, "We ought to build a..." Successes may have resulted, but usually only after a long, uncomfortable period of missed deadlines, overrun budgets and costly redesigns.

The critical tasks in the MAP process are the selection of which market needs to pursue and the detailed definitions of the products that match those needs. During the Needs Phase, the marketplace, technology, and business processes are studied and marketplace needs are targeted. During the Feasibility Phase, a quick study is conducted to determine if there are any obvious reasons not to continue the project. During the Definition Phase, that knowledge is transformed into the definition of a product that will successfully satisfy the marketplace.

The definition process is intended to have the desirable side effect of spreading a thorough understanding of the proposed product throughout the company. This eliminates much of the oversight that results in last minute changes and redesign. It's during the Definition Phase that customer need is balanced with the available technology and business processes.

"The biggest expense in product development is time," observes an executive with an electronics company. "If you're ready to go into production and discover a product definition problem, it costs you at least another generation of circuit boards, which is eight weeks, and that's eight weeks in the marketplace that you have lost. And if you're in a competitive marketplace, you can lose that time and be in a situation you might never recover from." It's even a double whammy: time was lost not only from the current product but also the next product, which has been delayed for the eight weeks its predecessor was held up.

That said, we've found product definition to be the most underrated and most poorly done phase of product development. At the very root of the problem in product definition are two issues—the pressure to quickly get the product into design, where we are traditionally more comfortable, and the inability to communicate well. We have designed a gate at the end of the definition process that addresses the first issue. A product can't get through the gate to the Design Phase until we have a good definition in hand—there are no short cuts!

Defining both the product and process before design begins results in fewer delays and change orders after production release. An additional bonus is that it speeds the actual cycle time to deliver quality product to the customer. Drawing upon the company's collective knowledge and experience, the quality and productivity are defined into the product. Then, when we're ready to go to the Design Phase, the product can be designed correctly the first time through, rather than redesigned by a series of change orders later.

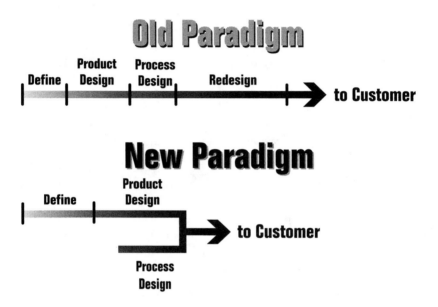

Too often, a product idea consisting of generalized statements only is launched into Design Phase because of our eagerness to get on with it. The unfortunate side effect of this rush to design is that we have lots of changes to make while the project is being completed, an unacceptable situation that results in schedule and budget overruns and product reliability problems.

Consider the example of painting a house cited by Dave Garwood and Michael Bane in their book, *Shifting Paradigms.* You and your spouse decide it's time to paint the house and you agree upon natural green. The painting contractor gives you a bid and gets the contract. As the house is being painted, you decide that a different natural green is better. Change order Number One is issued, and the contractor reluctantly says he can do that for only a little extra money. The delay won't be too long, either. After the trim is half completed, you decide that, rather than dark green, slate gray would be better. Change order Number Two, and the contractor reluctantly agrees and smiles on the way to the bank. After a while though, even the contractor tires of the changes and just wants to get the job done. As the paint ages, you begin to see the subtle color changes where the over painting occurred. The job ran over schedule, over budget, is of poor quality, and no one is happy.

> The biggest gains in efficiency will come from improving the definition of the new product.

The same effect happens in product development. Some changes are inevitable, because we know least about the project when we are first starting it. But many of the changes that do occur are avoidable. We often have advance access to much of the information that—because we haven't used it for one reason or another—creates the need for changes in midstream. In other words, changes are the result of information we could have laid our hands on, if we'd only thought to look. Under the MAP process, we thoroughly gather the information and prepare as detailed a definition as possible before starting the design. Since the relevant information will be communicated throughout the company, all departments need to be involved in the definition process.

Preparing a good definition before the design begins becomes even more important as the marketplace becomes more competitive. As we strive for World Class performance levels, we are speeding up the cycle time and running more things in parallel. When changes do occur, as we mentioned earlier, more resources and time have already been expended. A "pro" of the parallel process is that it does speed up the time-to-market cycle; a "con" is that changes have far-reaching affects on everyone.

Think about the development of a new product in terms of building a house. If a company's new product strategy is the foundation of the house, the Definition Phase is the framing. If the ideas selected to execute the strategy (the foundation) are flawed, everything that follows is going to be a series of patches and poorly thought out reactions, with less than optimum results. If the definition (the framing) is done incorrectly, we have suddenly entered a world of "REs"—rethink, rework, repair, and on and on. Usually after a significant amount of resources—the most precious of which is time—have been wasted, the flaws in the definition are discovered and the development effort has to be revisited and redone to some degree.

Defining Product And Process

Adjustments in the product and process during the Definition Phase make the product more producible and the processes more controllable. Consider the case of a commercial refrigerator. The refrigeration system rarely needs to be serviced, but when a problem occurs, the service must be prompt—or else. If the refrigeration system breaks down, thousands of dollars of perishable food will be lost if the problem is not corrected quickly. There are a couple of different approaches we can use to minimize our problems. We could schedule lots of maintenance visits, although, realistically, most of those will be wasted. A better idea might be to add a little computerization to the refrigeration unit— when the temperature fluctuates, the computer will "call home" and ask for a repair technician. We could add this feature after the fact, but how much more efficient to include it from the beginning. If we define this need in the beginning, we'll save time, money and probably a lot of design grief.

> We've found product definition to be the most underrated and most poorly done phase of product development.

Under the MAP process, we deal with the process and product questions in the Definition Phase. The process issues are ironed out at the same time as the product issues.

How To Define

The team leader who began managing the project in the Feasibility Phase continues to manage in the Definition Phase. This team leader can come from any department, but it's not unusual for the team leaders initially to come from the Engineering department. As you progress in the journey, team leaders will emerge from other departments. When the project passes through the gate at the end of the Feasibility Phase, the project leader begins to recruit—on a company-wide basis—the members of the team required to define the product.

> The actual definition begins with an "assumption list," which is a collection of thoughts about the product.

The actual definition begins with an "assumption list," which is a collection of thoughts about the product. It is important to note the list is not in any specific order. We have found through experience that the order of the list is not as important as just getting all the ideas down. The process is similar to brainstorming. You're looking for a quick, free flow of thoughts about the product. When people begin to worry about the order of the list, the flow of information slows to a trickle as time and energy is devoted to the "right order." First get everyone's thoughts on the table; let the sorting, deleting and organizing come later.

At this point, everyone is encouraged to contribute ideas, and people aren't restricted to their own areas of expertise. However, we ensure that people understand some basic roles so that important perspectives aren't overlooked.

The engineers are responsible for managing the product technology risks and opportunities. As the product is defined, the technology that will be used in developing the product is evaluated. It is the engineers' responsibility to ensure that the final definition of the product can indeed be executed. If, for example, we've decided to design a 10-pound fusion reactor and we don't have the technology required, this is the time and place for that fact to be noted.

This doesn't mean that we do not take technical risks. In almost every new product effort, some technology is required that is not at our fingertips. Engineering will have to "stretch" to meet the demands of the marketplace. Engineering ultimately has the task of deciding how much we can stretch and still end up with a realizable and reliable product.

As the detailed definition evolves, engineering masters an understanding of the product and the magnitude of the design effort. Using this knowledge, engineering estimates the project schedule and the development budget, and provides the estimates to the PDRB at the end of the Definition Phase.

Manufacturing is responsible for managing the process technology risks and opportunities and making sure the processes required to build the product are available internally or externally. If they're not available, Manufacturing must ensure that they can be developed while the product is being designed. If we are about to embark on a journey that requires the alchemist to turn lead into gold, it is Manufacturing's responsibility to point out the obstacles. They can't be totally risk-aversive, but the risk must be managed, and the first step to managing risk is to be aware of its existence. Ask any alchemist.

As the details of the product are clarified, Manufacturing helps Engineering estimate the gross margin the product will generate. Also, if any extraordinary capital expenditures are required to "tool up" for the product, Manufacturing summarizes the expenses.

Sales interfaces with and represents the customers to the company. They communicate the customers' wants, and also communicate what is being asked for on specific purchase orders. Sales people determine the innovative customers who should be involved directly in the definition of a specific product. They gather necessary information from the customers and input it into the marketing database. Sometimes, Sales is used as a sounding board to answer the question, "Can you sell this?"

Marketing represents the marketplace. The difference between the marketplace and the customer can be confusing. The customer is an individual person or a specific company. A market is a common issue that involves many customers. What a single individual wants may not be the same as what the majority of the customers need. While Sales is representing individuals and specific companies, Marketing must piece together the overall puzzle of what the marketplace, consisting of thousands (or more) of individuals, will purchase.

One reason that historically we have not done a good job on new product definition is that our marketing tools need to be augmented and updated. New marketing tools, like the S curve discussed in future chapters, are used to augment the life cycle concepts already popularized by the Boston Consulting Group and Harvard Business School.

> The idea, remember, is not to eliminate the conflict.

Marketing, with help from Sales, estimates the sales revenues expected from the proposed product during its first five years. This information is usually arrived at by setting a sales price target and estimating the sales volume for each of the first five years.

Finance looks at the new product proposals in terms of the development budgets, projected revenues, gross margins and the financial structure of the company. In short, the financial people look for compatibility with the existing financial structure of the company and highlight any areas that need to be reviewed in detail. If the company has characteristically spent 35 percent of sales on purchased materials and the new product proposal outlines a plan to spend 50 percent of sales on purchased material, the reason needs to be investigated. Not taking care of these trends early on can result in some nasty surprises later.

Product service must define the service strategy for the new product. Will it be serviced in a service center or will it be serviced on the customer's site? Will a phone modem link be built into the product? Would remote diagnostics improve the productivity of the service organization? With all these people defining the product, working together is not synonymous with total agreement—there will be conflict. The idea, remember, is not to eliminate the conflict. Rather, you need to provide forums to optimally resolve the conflicts that naturally exist. This "creative conflict" is actually healthy. It causes the company to stretch.

In the ideal forum, Engineering signs up to do more than the existing technology allows, but not more than they can execute with diligent effort. Marketing signs up to work harder—and smarter—to determine which features and functions are really required and which are superfluous. They do this by studying the market and getting closer to the customer. Sales signs up to overcome some of the customer's objections that arise because of wants rather than needs. They learn the customer's business and your products. They practice presentations and work on proposals that emphasize satisfying the customer's need rather than getting into the features and functions war.

> **When conflict is focused on business issues, it is healthy.**

Our suppliers will not necessarily be on the same path we're traveling. They may see us as trying to dominate their businesses—the ugliest and least productive connotation of "partnership."

We may conflict with collaborating companies on strategy and tactics—and even goals.

Finally, we may, at times, be at odds with our customers over form and function, needs versus wants. But in each case, there exists the potential for us to use the successful resolution of those conflicts to our advantage.

The challenge is to define the product well enough that it will be successful and there will be no surprises. This requires everyone on the team to represent their particular expertise during the process. That does not necessarily mean that every decision is a consensus decision. There are natural conflicts between the department goals. Conflict is even encouraged, up to—and not including—personal attack. When conflict is focused on business issues, it is healthy, but when it becomes personal, it is destructive.

To achieve resolution, some of the differences may require intervention by the Product Development Review Board or, ultimately, the company CEO. The conflicts and decision-making process must be an above-board, on the table process that the team members can see, participate in and understand, because everyone is expected to support the final decision.

The Product Use Scenario

Once we have an understanding of the customer's true needs, and we have an understanding of state of the art methods and technologies, we need to meld the two into a new product definition.

At this point, the use of product scenarios to discuss the proposed new product comes into play. The concept is to study, document and communicate the essence of the customer's business, the technology and the methods used to fulfill needs by documenting the scenarios in which a potential product will be used. Using a scenario approach gets us out of the no-win battle of features and functions and moves us closer to a more productive awareness of how the new product actually solves a problem or fulfills a need.

In 1985, I. C. Marc of IBM described the scenario technique in *Research and Development* magazine. The concept is simple; it requires some work to apply. The idea is to realistically describe the way a product will be used: step-by-step, paint a moving picture of the exact way a product will be set up, used, serviced, and so forth.

For example, suppose that you're going to develop a product designed to help people sort and hold their garbage for recycling. Based on studies of the customer's need, you have acquired extensive information about the situation. You know what garbage is going to be recycled, how often and when the garbage is picked up, items the customer must take to recycling centers vs. material the local garbage collection service will pick up, new or pending recycling laws, etc. The product designers will know the materials that can be used to build containers, how much weight certain materials can support, how much the average person can lift, etc.

By graphically building the scenario using the new product, the customer's need is integrated with the available methods and technology. The creation of the scenario might start something like this:

A marketing person points out that the average household receives eight newspapers a week, resulting in an "X-inch" stack, weighing "X pounds."

Brainstorming off this observation, someone else suggests that magazines need to be taken into account. This brings up the question about what type of paper will be accepted at the recycling center. A product designer observes that the average person can safely lift about "Y" pounds, and suggests that the container should be capable of holding just one weeks' worth of newspapers.

The designer also notes that his suggestion is well within the capability of the plastics being used in the fabrication of similar containers.

Someone else suggests that the plastic collected from the recycled waste could be used to fabricate the containers, which would provide a great public relations opportunity. Another marketing person notes that often the recycling containers are provided by the collection company and are not purchased by individuals.

It is also noted that some recycling companies want the newspapers tied in a bundle with string. The product designer suggests the container might be designed to allow the newspapers to be tied with string after being placed in the container.

And the brainstorming/mixing of need with technology continues until agreement is reached. The final scenario for the recycling containers may look something like this: The newspapers will be collected and stored in a plastic basket that is _____ by _____ by _____ high. The papers will normally be collected for _____weeks resulting in a total container weight of _____ pounds. A separate basket for magazines will be provided that will be _____ by _____ by _____ high. The magazines will normally be collected for _____weeks resulting in a total weight of _____pounds.

The containers will be designed so the newspapers and magazines can be tied in a bundle with string while in the container.

It will be recommended that the customer keep and reuse any paper bags they receive during shopping. (This recommendation will be used later as a "green" statement in the product introduction and sales program.) It will also be suggested that other types of paper waste, such as used paper towels, be disposed of in the regular garbage because no recyclers currently accept them.

The same scenario technique would be used to describe the containers for cans (aluminum or steel), glass, plastic, etc. The designer's suggestion to use recycled plastic for the containers can itself be recycled and applied to the additional plans. This type of discussion leads to a fuller understanding of the product and how the customer will use it.

The scenario activity leads to a comprehensive knowledge base on which to build sales presentations that will appeal to the customer because they demonstrate a high level of understanding and leadership.

The scenario technique also forces us to participate in a thorough review of the new product definition. All too often, overlooked details emerge after the product is already in production. Worse yet, someone knew about the important detail in advance, but there was no forum in which to pass on that knowledge and have it incorporated into the product definition.

In addition, when the scenario technique is properly facilitated, the discussions stay focused on factual information rather than personal opinion. Every company will develop its own approach to the selection and definition of new products. However, the basic theme of understanding needs, technology and business processes—and using scenarios—is hard to beat.

The Communication Challenge

Communication remains the most difficult challenge. The problem is that it is easy to talk in generalities, but it is difficult to get people to see the same product vision. Because it is not easy, the temptation is to take advantage of the illusion that communication has taken place when, in fact, it has not. As a folk singer once sang, "Let the path of least resistance lead me on..."

Communication is always a challenge in the definition process. In working with companies, I never cease to be amazed at how many product development projects are launched on definitions such as, "We are going to build the best..." The problem with statements like building the "best" is that the "best" is in the eye of the beholder, and no real communication has occurred. Worst of all, there is the illusion that communication has occurred.

If you are making a presentation to executive decision-makers in an auto manufacturing company, you will get immediate agreement that the goal is to make the "best" car available. But what does that mean, really? Value judgments, vague adjectives and intangibles replace concrete, tangible facts and observations. But people can agree on something as obvious as the goal being to make the "best;" so, thinking that all is well, they move on to the task of acting on their view of the situation.

> Worst of all, there is the illusion that communication has occurred.

The problem is that the individual views of "best" will differ greatly: the financial person would think that the "best" car is a car with a list price of $20,000 and a 70 percent gross margin. The sales person, who is a charter subscriber to *Car and Driver* magazine, thinks the "best" car is painted candy apple red and named after an exotic animal. It goes zero to 60 mph in two seconds and corners on a dime. The environmental affairs representative thinks she's signed up for a car that gets 400 miles per gallon. And last, but not least, the aces from Engineering think the "best" is a technological marvel, with heads-up technology that makes the driver's display look like the cockpit of an F-16.

If, after the agreement is reached to build the "best" car, the engineers go out and design the technological marvel, a lot of people are going to be surprised, and few will be happy. The project is destined to undergo many changes in midstream, as people belatedly discover the misunderstanding.

Words and expressions like best, same-as-but-better, improved, state of the art, leading edge, etc., are dangerous. While our hypothetical car company may seem (and is) an overstated example, you need only look at the field of personal computers, especially software development, to see this scenario repeated again and again. More than one company has set out to write the best word processor program or the best spreadsheet program. Millions of lines of code later, there are numerous expensive surprises and no one is happy. The kludged-together programs that do make it to the shelves just sit there, gathering dust.

Defining a product in user's terms guarantees a forum is provided for everyone's participation.

Communication is difficult for other reasons as well. The vocabulary and interests of the various professions differ. The many people involved in the Definition Phase also have regular responsibilities and, at times, it's difficult to get them to work on a project that has a longer-term deadline than their routine duties, and might not be available for many months (although, a few years ago, that sentence would have read, not be available for years).

In order to facilitate the communication process, we also discourage the use of design requirements or design criteria couched in technical terms. Trouble is brewing when the primary means of communicating with the Marketing, Sales, Finance and other non-engineering people is a thick design "brief" that demonstrates the Engineers' advanced vocabulary. The brief is seldom fully read and never fully conveys the product concept. A good, in-depth technical design brief is more powerful than sleeping pills for the exact people who you most need to keep not only awake, but also interested and involved in the definition process.

Part of our solution has been to use a vocabulary in which everyone shares an interest: the customer's vocabulary.

Everyone in the company must be interested in the customer. Defining a product in user's terms guarantees that the communication process is interesting and that a forum is provided for everyone's participation.

In addition to user's terms, fast prototypes are used to enhance the communication. There is no better way to communicate the size, shape, color or weight of a proposed new product, than to build a quick model. Passing a model around the conference room table communicates more in a few minutes than written words can communicate in days.

The Gate

The gate at the end of the Definition Phase is more quantitative and qualitative than the gate at the end of the Needs or Feasibility phases. The project team has studied the many facets of the proposed product and has estimated schedules, sales volumes for each of the first five years in the Launch Phase, sales prices, target costs, schedule to complete design, gross margin and quality issues. When the definition is complete, it is presented to the PDRB. The product proposal is reviewed for completeness and compatibility with the company's strategy and tactics. The development budget and schedule is compared with the gross margin estimates and the projected sales revenue.

If the product proposal is in concert with the PDRB's understanding of the company's position in the marketplace, and the financial numbers make sense, the project is approved to move through the gate into the Design Phase. If there is a minor problem area, the PDRB may ask that the proposal be reviewed and modified to remedy the problem. Sometimes the budget and the revenue projections make it clear that the product will not be a success, the project is dropped, and a new marketplace need is chosen to pursue. If there are other problems so large that further definition effort will not help, the project may also be canceled and a new idea is selected from the needs list.

Chapter 8

Phase Four: Design

During the Design Phase, the detailed definition of the product is converted into the information required for the company to sell, order, produce and service the product. In addition to creation of the product prototype, this phase is where the support materials and knowledge are developed and brought together under the product's umbrella. This ancillary information is as integral to the product's success as the product itself, and provides the complete overview of the product—everything that's necessary to bring the product to market, ranging from fabrication drawings to the instruction manual. The Design Phase is the formalizing of the knowledge that—primarily through documentation—is used to order parts, manufacture, test, etc. Representative of the deliverables produced in this phase are:
- Fabrication drawings
- Test procedures
- Bills of material
- Manufacturing process instructions
- Service documentation

- Service tools
- Ordering information
- Catalog data
- Application notes
- Sales training programs
- Customer training programs

Product and Process

A recurring theme throughout the MAP process is to design the processes at the same time we design the product. The reason is simple—all the various elements are interrelated. The order entry process, for example, has a significant affect on sales productivity and effectiveness. If the product is designed in a way that requires a laborious and error-prone order entry process, a rough road lies ahead. Sales will either have to live with the results or try to get the product redesigned—neither a pleasant prospect.

> A recurring theme throughout the MAP process is to design the processes at the same time we design the product.

Sales might be able to improve sales productivity by using personal computers in the order entry process. That, however, presupposes that the product design enables an order entry process compatible with personal computers. The same premise holds true for all the other aspects of the new product. If the product is software, are we delivering on disks, CD-ROM or on-line? If the product is a seminar, in which cities do we plan to deliver? All these other processes must be designed parallel to the product itself to guarantee a seamless presentation.

One of the most thought-provoking concepts of designing salability into a product is the chemical distributor who developed a cellular phone module that attaches to a 55-gallon drum filled with their product. As the product is depleted, the drum "calls home" and reports the situation. The distributor has contracts with his customers agreeing that the call is authorization to deliver another 55- gallon drum, applying it to a blanket purchase order. The distributor has low sales overhead; the customer has low inventory and doesn't have to worry about materials planning. This is the classic example of a win/win situation.

Designing a product that is manufacturable may be easy to talk about and agree upon, but it is often difficult to actualize. First, the quality must be designed in. This is another concept that's readily accepted in general terms, but frequently not understood in terms that allow it to be accomplished. Let's look at an example that defines the concept in more concrete terms and demonstrates the evolution in the meaning of "quality" from the 1970s to now.

The example is a new product that includes a two-piece injected molded case. In the 1970s, the design might have called for the case to be fastened together with four screws of different lengths. The design functioned and was considered a success.

However, consider the situation in which the design placed the Manufacturing people: they had to purchase four different length screws, stock four different screws and kit four different screws for assembly. Worst of all, the people on the assembly line had to work very hard to get the right screws in the right place.

Inevitably, out of the thousands of cases that were assembled, a screw would be misplaced, resulting in a defective product. The quality thought process of the 1970s—that paradigm—was that the people were just not trying hard enough. If they just cared, they would be careful and get it right. Meanwhile, strain built up for the people on the assembly line, and the relationship between management and the line worker degenerated into mutual disrespect.

This no-win situation worsened even further when manufacturing tried to get the design changed. The injection molds, used to produce the case piece, quite likely cost $50,000 or more. The screws cost a few cents. Trying to justify the expenditure of another $50,000 to save money on the screws that cost pennies was impossible. Literally, the die was already cast.

Quality From The Ground Up

Now we know that the quality solution is to have Manufacturing involved in the design from Day One. If given the opportunity, Manufacturing can suggest using one type of screw in all four locations. When the quality is designed in, very frequently improved productivity is also designed in. With this design, only one type of screw actually needed to be purchased, stocked, etc. Best of all, it is far easier to assemble the product correctly. The strain on the assembly people is reduced, and at least one more source of tension between the company's line people and management is eliminated.

Using actual processes to order, plan and build the prototypes allows us to actually kill two birds with one stone.

There are many other ways the design of the product has a profound affect on the manufacturing processes and vice versa. For example, if we are designing a part that will be handled by a robot, the shape of the part will determine how easy it is for the robot to pick up the part and properly position it. If the robot's capabilities are not considered when the part is designed, it may be very difficult to automate the handling of the part.

Making the product manufacturable means designing in the quality and productivity from the outset. Manufacturing engineers and the people who work in manufacturing are the obvious experts on processes used to manufacture the product; these people must be involved in the Design Phase.

Product Service has a role similar to manufacturing and sales. Product Service puts together the product service plan and participates in the product design to ensure serviceability. Perhaps phone modem capability, discussed earlier, is required for the product to call home when it gets sick. Maybe it's a simple matter of making the critical test points easily accessible, or just making the product easy to disassemble and repair. Low tech or high tech, the service plan and the product must be synergistic.

During the Design Phase, Marketing creates the launch package. The term launch plan has been used by Allen Bradley for some time. It's basically a collection of written material to help effectively take the product to market. There are many different components of a launch plan, including:

- Sales briefing
- Launch schedule
- Product description and/or data sheets
- Trade show plans
- Application information
- Potential questions about the product and suggested answers
- Potential customer profiles
- Customer training plans and programs
- Competitive product information and competitive analysis
- Sales training plans and programs

This material should be completed and ready for distribution by the time the product is ready for the marketplace—preferably before.

Engineering designs the product. There are volumes of literature on product design that need not be repeated here. But there are some practices directly related to the MAP process that warrant discussion.

During the Design Phase, the product is prototyped and tested to ensure that it complies with the definition and performs reliably. The processes used to order, manufacture and test the product are also tested. Using actual processes to order, plan and build the prototypes allows us to actually kill two birds with one stone: the prototypes get built and the processes are tested at the same time.

Build Where You Run

There are major advantages to building the prototypes in the manufacturing unit. The primary advantage is the manufacturing processes can be prototyped at the same time the product is prototyped. Manufacturing also gets to "test-drive" the new product, evaluating manufacturability at the point changes can still be made. They also get to check all associated documents, such as bills of material, routings, test specifications and the like. Our goal is always to design the product right the first time and not require changes even during the prototyping activities, but changes during the Design Phase are far easier to make than after production release.

> The loading process begins before the bills are complete.

Building prototypes in Manufacturing can actually be quicker than the hand-crafted approach. If the engineering database is "integrated" with the manufacturing database, prototypes can be built cost-effectively on automated equipment. The resulting speed with which prototypes can be built could only be dreamed about a few years ago. Occasionally difficulties arise when prototyping in the actual manufacturing environment, but doing it this way heads off a much higher price than if we don't.

During design, the bills of material are loaded into the computer. The loading process begins before the bills are complete, and this information is used by the manufacturing planning people to procure the materials required for prototypes. A "futures flag" is used to identify the bills of material as a non-released product so the planners can make appropriate lot-size decisions.

Loading the bills of material into the scheduling system has a second advantage. The master schedule for the product is loaded before the product is released for production so procurement and lower level fabrication and assembly can start prior to production release. The new product schedule is reviewed and the initial production rate is planned at the Sales and Operations Planning meeting to support beta test units, sales demonstration units and customer requirements. This pre-planning reduces the time lag between design completion and delivery to the marketplace.

When the product is not a manufactured item—such as a service or other non-widget item—we still have a "bill of material," the complete list of all the items that go into that particular service. All the above rules apply.

Be Willing To Go Outside

In the face of today's specialty niches and frenzied pace, much of the technological or process expertise essential to maintaining a competitive edge may not exist within your company. The necessary knowledge and/or skills may reside in a another company or institution. Whether internal or external, however, you want to involve the experts with their skills and knowledge in the product development process from Day One. If it is external, therefore, you must develop a fruitful relationship with this supplier of knowledge, products and/or processes.

I often have heard the argument that new products are too sensitive to involve people from outside the company early on. But, if the expertise you require in order to be the high-quality, low-cost producer resides in an outside resource, you have a choice:

1) Learn the process yourself, which takes precious time.

2) Sacrifice optimum quality and cost.

3) Involve the supplier.

The optimum choice is to involve a trusted supplier.

The bar code industry provides a good case history of how the use of a product from an outside company helped to give one fast-moving company the competitive edge.

Bar code companies realized about the same time as one another that wireless communication of bar code data would be very useful in many situations. Data that was bar coded in a warehouse could be updated in the central computer on a real-time basis if the data were radioed to the computer from on-site rather than waiting for the portable terminal to be carried to a fixed location and plugged in for transmission.

The optimum choice is to involve a trusted supplier.

One bar code company, Intermec, contacted sources already in the radio and data telemetry industry and had them apply their existing knowledge to quickly develop a product. As a result, Intermec was able to get the product to market quickly, before many of its competitors.

Being able to take advantage of the advanced technologies of other companies before your competition can requires a close working relationship with key suppliers. You want to actually invite them to join your development team. If you don't invite them into the inner sanctum, you must be prepared to learn the technology and then apply it to the product development process. This serial approach is time-consuming and never as efficient as directly involving the in-depth experience of the seasoned professional.

You may still develop much of the technology, but it's important to keep asking yourself, "Are we reinventing the wheel?" What we should be asking is, "Are the areas we are spending time and resources on differentiating us from the competition?"

Because of questions like this, Bently Nevada Corporation decided to discontinue the chemical processes associated with the fabrication of printed wiring boards. (These are the boards to which components are added and soldered in place, creating functional electrical circuits.) Bently Nevada had fabricated its own printed wiring boards since very early in the company's history. However, the time had come to invest significant capital resources to bring the manufacturing process up to state-of-the-art levels. Since the company was spending a large portion of its management time on the issues of compliance with the new laws and regulations regarding chemicals, we decided to study the situation rather than automatically proceed with the upgrade. After determining that many suppliers could produce the printed wiring boards at or below the internal manufacturing cost, with comparable quality, we decided to put the company's time and effort into other areas that would more definitively differentiate us from the competition.

Even though the process of fabricating the circuit boards was moved to external organizations, the suppliers' process experts were required to participate in the development process and to advise on the design practices that would most effectively maximize quality and minimize cost. Some of the benefits realized through optimization were used to boost the supplier's margins; some were used to lower Bently Nevada's costs. This is the way win/win partnerships are supposed to work.

More On Quality

Our goal, remember, is defect-free designs. To accomplish this, we must design the product right the first time. Most design errors that cause poor quality are the result of lack of knowledge, not the lack of desire.

One way to assure design quality is through design reviews. In a design review, the team leader presents the design to either the PDRB or an engineering team, which, in effect, function as "inspectors." The design reviews have two purposes: they serve as a teaching tool, and they inspect for design errors. Reviews are most effective as a teaching tool. The second purpose—reviewing the quality into a design—is analogous to inspecting quality into the manufacture of a product. Inspection is only going to catch a certain percentage of the errors, and the others are going to pass through to haunt you at a later date. It does not address root causes.

Providing people with the knowledge enabling them to design something right the first time is the best path to defect-free design. The concept of "corporate knowledge" vs. "individual knowledge" is the key. Much of our learning process is empirical, meaning that the experience of making a mistake is the teacher. Most professionals are good individual learners—they learn from their past mistakes and don't repeat them. Effective product development requires that people not only learn from their mistakes, but also from the mistakes of others. The goal of corporate learning is to have everyone learn from each others' mistakes, so the company doesn't repeat errors. Logs of previous errors serve as good corporate learning tools. These logs may simply be a chronological list of problems that have occurred in the past, which are

> Most design errors that cause poor quality are the result of lack of knowledge, not the lack of desire.

reviewed as part of the new product process. Another tool is a check list of issues that are important and must be considered for every product or process.

The team leader must use several techniques to manage the Design Phase. During the Design Phase, the team leader has historically reported to Engineering or Marketing. The report protocol is not important; the need for the team leader to receive coaching and direction on project management techniques is.

Risk Management

Risk management in the Design Phase is critical. Unless the risks are well managed at the beginning of the Design Phase, time and resources are wasted on issues that will change when more significant or less controllable challenges arise. Second only to poor or incomplete definitions, poor risk management is the cause of overruns. When problems are "discovered" late in the design, last minute recovery activities result in cost overruns, schedule overruns and product quality problems. Early time spent on the wrong issues is usually wasted.

The rule is "difficult and inflexible items first."

The situation can be visualized by considering the design of a mass-produced, low-cost house. Suppose the door jambs are designed before the size of standard doors is considered. When it is "discovered" that expensive custom doors will be required, the design will have to be redone. The redesign effort is further complicated when it is "discovered" that changing the size of the doors causes unacceptable changes in the floor plan. This is a simple—although highly probable—example, and it graphically illustrates the necessity of addressing issues in the correct order. Risk management is largely determining what must be done first so what follows will fall neatly into place, and what is simpler or more flexible and should be done later. The rule is "difficult and inflexible items first."

During the Definition Phase, fast prototype techniques are used to assess the highest risk facets of the product. The fast prototyping usually carries over into the beginning of the Design Phase. Fast prototyping is the modeling of a portion of a product both to learn what is possible, and to use as a communication tool. For example, it's easier and more useful to hand someone an object of a specific weight than to say, "It weighs five pounds." Caution must be used here not to complicate fast prototypes. Complicated fast prototypes that use a significant amount of resources are self-defeating, often using more time and resources than they save.

Communication

As the number of people involved increases, the number of possible communications links increase proportionately and rapidly. In fact, the number of communication paths increase geometrically with the addition of people to the new product equation.

One way to control the number of communication paths is to establish "standard interfaces" between subgroups in the team.

The next graphic shows how such an interface significantly reduces the number of time consuming links.

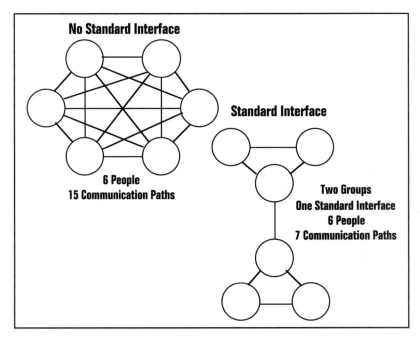

No Standard Interface

6 People
15 Communication Paths

Standard Interface

Two Groups
One Standard Interface
6 People
7 Communication Paths

The team leader determines where standard interfaces should be established in the internal team. Suppose a project involves both hardware and software. A decision must be made to organize the interface between the hardware and software people or informally leave it up to the team members. The team leader never tells the team members not to talk to each other, but rather decides where interfaces will be defined very early in the design, facilitating the communication requirement.

> Any single step, or mission, should take no longer than three months to accomplish.

An example of a standard interface existing in almost all companies is the relationship with suppliers. In this case, the first link in the standard interface is the supplier's product specification or data sheet. Instead of everyone in one company trying to communicate with everyone in the supplier's organization, the required information is communicated in writing through documents such as data sheets or product specifications.

In addition to the documents, specific people are designated as the standard interface to represent a company—sales representatives, for example, or marketing, traffic or production coordinators or liaisons.

The supplier example offers another insight to standard interfaces—specifically when not to use them. If the supplier's standard product needs to be modified to optimize your project, data sheets and product specifications will not suffice. In addition, the communication task is likely to be of such technical depth that sales people can actually hinder accurate communication. Under these conditions, communication must be established directly with the supplier's designers, calling in your company's engineers or manufacturing experts.

Manufacturing specifications are an important form of standard interface—it's not productive to have all the design engineers learn all of the manufacturing processes. Likewise, it's not beneficial to have the process expert from manufacturing be on every design team. The solution is to create standard manufacturing specifications for certain processes.

Mission Statements

Another technique used to manage the design process is to break down the process into a series of short time frame mission statements. Any single step, or mission, should take no longer than three months to accomplish. These short mission statements keep us in touch with the timeliness of activities and help keep overruns from accumulating. It's much better to develop the discipline of periodically doing whatever is necessary to stay on schedule rather than getting into the habit of "making up the time" in the next step. Project leaders can monitor progress with expenditure charts, time-line schedules and major milestones.

Tools

The choice of tools is a major influence on the effectiveness of the Design Phase. In the 1970s and 80s, a plethora of products claimed to improve the productivity of the product development process. Powerful computers were going to save us all. Unfortunately, many of these so-called "productivity" tools required more effort to run than effort saved. The bottom line productivity gains never materialized. However, these early efforts did give birth to many tools that evolved and, in combination with the low-cost of computing power in today's personal computers, have begun to deliver the promised gains.

In the new product development paradigm, design tools can create databases used in ordering, manufacturing, delivering and servicing the product.

The computerized pattern layout tool for the garment designer, for example, downloads its database directly to the laser cloth-cutter. The printed circuit board design system downloads its database to the computer-controlled circuit board drills, computerized photo plotters and the other automated equipment used to build circuit boards.

The key is to select tools based on what they can do to optimize your process, rather than because they're the latest release with the most hyperbolic promises.

The Gate

Up to this point, the gates have all been controlled by the PDRB. The gate at the end of the Design Phase, however, is controlled by the team members. Engineering reviews the test results; Marketing reviews the launch package; Quality Assurance reviews the design; Manufacturing reviews the status of the fabrication and test processes; Product Service checks to be sure the product can be serviced. When the team members agree that the design is complete and the issues involving their various departments have been resolved, they "production release" the product. This is a joint statement by all the team members that the product is ready to be sold, manufactured, delivered and supported in a manner that will meet the customer's expectations and successfully compete in the marketplace. After passing the Design Gate, the product enters the Launch Phase.

Chapter 9

Phase Five: Launch

The Launch Phase begins after the product passes through the design gate and ends after the agreed-upon timeframe—for example, two to four years—has elapsed. After the Launch Phase, the product is considered mature, graduated out of the new product process.

This period has been referred to as "after release," and historically, has tended to be open ended, with no set timeframe. Like any of the other phases, it's a mistake to think the launch will take care of itself.

During the launch, the sales training efforts and customer training efforts are carried out. The product is scheduled and built in production quantities, and the progress and performance of the product is tracked in the field.

The tendency is to short-change the Launch Phase, which is a serious mistake. The Launch Phase is as important as any other phase.

"If you look at product development in terms of phases, you can die in any phase," says one executive. "You can define the right product, engineer the right product, build the right product, then not make any money because your distribution process wasn't ready for it."

The gate at the beginning of the Launch Phase is the first gate not managed by the PDRB.

In the MAP process, the Launch Phase continues until the learning and enhancement processes of the product have stabilized. Minor iterations of existing products tend to stabilize fairly rapidly, but a brand new product concept may take many years before the Launch Phase is complete.

The gate at the beginning of the Launch Phase is the first gate not managed by the PDRB. As discussed in the previous chapter, the product passes through the gate when the team members from the various departments determine it is ready to be sold, manufactured, delivered and serviced. That is, Engineering believes the product design is defect-free, Manufacturing believes the processes are defect-free, Marketing believes the launch plan is complete, and the other departments are "ready."

Who Does What?

During the Launch Phase, Marketing carries out the launch plan. As part of the launch plan, the use of demonstration units is scheduled. The number of demonstration units was planned and master scheduled during the Design Phase. As the demonstration units are completed, they are routed to trade shows, customer presentations, sales offices and other critical "show and tell" activities.

Marketing also starts intensive training with the sales people. In some cases, the training is done as a traveling road show, where trainers travel to various satellite sites to impart their knowledge. Under other circumstances, the training is handled simply through the distribution of written documentation and training materials. Other products demand centralized training at one of the company's facilities. The objective is the same, however: to familiarize people with the product, the customer's need, how the need is fulfilled, and the status of competitive products.

The training department also starts the customer training during the Launch Phase. The objective of this training is very similar to the training of the sales force—familiarization with the product and the need it fulfills.

Sales actually begins selling the product during this phase— the reality and effectiveness of the new product development process really gets the acid test when Sales finally "asks for the order." If the customer is willing to give us that order, we've passed the test. If not, a distant—but useful—next best thing is to use the information and experience we've acquired during the process to refine our understanding of the marketplace. When our customers have reservations about the product, those reservations serve as basic clues to achieve success in the next generation of products.

For the same reasons, we also want our sales people to be gathering real world data on the performance of the product in the field. Hopefully, our efforts will result in some success stories that can be pulled together as case histories and circulated both inside and outside the company.

> When our customers have reservations about the product, those reservations serve as basic clues for the next generation.

In addition to direct customer training, the advertising program is activated, and the trade show presentations are coordinated and implemented.

Manufacturing produces and delivers the product. The performance of the product in the field is monitored, and appropriate adjustments—if necessary—in the manufacturing process are made. The Finance department helps Manufacturing track the cost of the product, making improvements as opportunities become available. Manufacturing establishes a method (or methods) to measure the quality of the product, and quality-related issues receive the highest priority.

The Service department carries out the service plan. The spare parts inventory is built up. The Service people are trained on the product and the failure analysis system is established. The objective is to retrieve every failed product and analyze what happened. It speaks well for a company if the failure rate is low enough that we can retrieve every problem product and analyze the situation to determine if action is required. We don't just fix a product and return it; we strive to understand the root cause. The continual learning that results keeps us in a formidable competitive position.

> A product is considered defective when it does not perform as defined.

Engineering remains involved with the product during the Launch Phase. Usually one of the up and coming engineers remains with the product. At one time, engineers considered it undesirable to support a product after it was being manufactured and sold. However, we have learned to appreciate the experience an individual gains during this phase. People who have been successful at supporting a product during the Launch Phase understand the value of designing defect-free products with the right features and functions the first time. It is now considered an opportunity and a career-building experience for an engineer to be involved with a new product in the Launch Phase.

The Engineer's Role

To understand the engineer's role during launch, the terms defect and enhancement must be clarified. A product is considered defective when it does not perform as defined, or the supporting documents contain errors. A manual containing an inaccurate statement, therefore, is considered a defect.

A product is said to require an enhancement when the product definition needs to be corrected to fulfill the customer's need. If we were developing a new automobile, for example, and the definition called for the car to get 20 miles to the gallon, and the new car obtained 21 miles to the gallon, the product would not be considered defective. However, if customers demanded 30 miles to the gallon before they would purchase the car, we would say the product needs an enhancement.

The engineer's first priority is to fix defects. If a defect is suspected, engineering investigates the situation. If a defect is discovered, it is fixed immediately—a big step in corporate learning. No other activity receives priority over fixing a defect. All other activities are set aside until the defect is fixed, period! Of course, the immediate next step is to discover the root cause of the defect and make sure it doesn't happen again.

The second priority for the engineer is to manage the enhancement requirements. All enhancement requests are documented. The enhancement requests are some of the best marketing information we can obtain for the next generation products as we move up the S curve. Enhancements are prioritized and implemented as resources become available. Seldom, actually never, are all enhancements implemented. But those essential to fulfilling the customer's needs must be implemented for the product to be successful.

Learn The Lessons

A common theme we've touched on again and again is the need for "corporate learning" as opposed to "individual learning." Your company may employ thousands of people with many different geographical locations involved in conducting the company's business. It is not acceptable, nor possible, for everyone to experience every lesson for themselves. Mistakes would be repeated too often, and successes could not be leveraged by the whole company.

Several methods have been established to pass on the learning experiences to everyone in the corporation. For example, if someone discovers that a particular electronic component is unreliable, the information is recorded in an engineering log. The log is used to train new engineers and is reviewed by experienced engineers to accumulate other individuals' experiences. With the modern information database management tools now available for even personal computers, the task of translating individual learning into "corporate learning" is becoming easier and more efficient.

Negative experiences can be used to determine what corrective action needs to be taken to prevent reoccurrence of the problem. If you're following the MAP process, however, you'll minimize the negative experiences by using effective measurements and tools to learn how to do it better the next time. The sales revenues are compared to the original estimates to determine how well we are progressing at planning new products. The elapsed time required to design products is measured and tracked to determine if the desired progress is occurring in the design methodology.

Supply And Demand

In order for the product to be available to the customer during the Launch Phase, the demand and the supply must be pre-planned. This can be accomplished by using the sales forecast documented in the Definition Phase, and by including the new product in the Sales and Operations Planning process. (The SOP process is the formal method used to balance customer requirements with production capabilities.)

Time To Develop The Next Product

In the MAP process, as we discussed, the Launch Phase ends when the learning and enhancement processes for the product have stabilized.

The length of the Launch Phase varies from product to product. Two criteria are used to determine when to move from launch to routine sustaining activities. First, the product must be defect-free. All known defects must have been corrected and field experience must indicate that no remaining defects exist. The second factor used to determine when a product should be moved out of launch is the market activity. When the questions on the use of the product and the request for enhancements to the product reaches a previously agreed upon level, it's time to move the product to sustaining. When a product transfers from launch to sustaining, it is transferred out of the new product development activity. By then the team's acquired knowledge is already being applied to the next new product.

Chapter 10

Toolbox: People

With a solid understanding of the phases and gates, we can move to the MAP Installation Toolbox. These are the "tools" we'll be using to implement the MAP process at our own company.

One of the first critical components is the new product development team and the team leader.

Ideally, the team leader should wear a blue body suit with a big red "S" on the chest under his or her business suit and have an affinity for phone booths.

Okay, maybe that's a bit extreme, but there's a reason for thinking that. The essential components of a good team leader are rare, and, as such, need to be cultivated.

For a start, team leaders can come from any of the company's departments. In the past, the tendency has been to choose team leaders from either Engineering or Marketing, largely as a reflection of the mistaken idea that new product development was the province of one of those two departments. As the MAP process spreads development chores across the company structure, and the strengths of other departments are recognized, team leaders will emerge from other departments. This process happens naturally—it's isn't necessary to go on a crusade to find team leaders from every department. Encourage the process; don't mandate it.

One strategy used in a company that adopted MAP has been to create a pool of potential team leaders from all the departments, each one qualified as a "general manager" of a product development team. As the resources become available, the company "dips" into the pool for the next team leader.

The Right Leader

What makes a good team leader?

• First and foremost, that person has to be a real leader, that is, a person who understands the MAP process and decides the right things to do in terms of the MAP process. Notice that the leader doesn't select which products to develop—that's a function of company strategic planning and market needs. But the leader needs to buy into the underlying philosophy of the process:

—that it's correct to have all departments represented

—that the phases and gates system is a good way to weed out

Characteristics of Team Leader

- **Strong leadership skills**
- **Good communicator**
- **Has executive management's confidence**
- **Credibility**
- **Persistence**
- **Understands strategic goals**

misdirected products

—that the methodology, if strictly adhered to, will yield the best results for the company and the customers.

The team leader must then have the personal strength not to violate those principles, regardless of pressure from management, other team members or even customers. Like we said, blue body suit and big, red "S."

As the project nears completion and the last few—usually unforeseen—problems still looming large, the team leader has to be able to rally the troops to solve those problems.

• A good team leader needs to be both an organizer and a communicator. He or she must be able to break the project down into digestible pieces, then communicate what needs to be done to the appropriate team members. The team leader needs to communicate that vision we talked about in the earliest chapters, the underlying philosophy behind the new product development efforts, to the team. Under the MAP process, it's very important to have a team leader who listens effectively, understands the actual circumstances and can facilitate the solution.

> Team leaders can come from any of the company's departments.

• The team leader must also have the confidence of the management team. This is because our team leader may have to deliver bad news. When the pressure is on to release a new product still suffering from design problems, the team leader must have the absolute credibility that will enable him or her to delay that release. Of course, the team leader has to then be able to deliver.

• The team leader needs to have that same credibility with all the members of the team as well as management. With so many people involved, there are bound to be disagreements—if there weren't, something would definitely be wrong! The team leader must be able to facilitate a resolution to the conflicts. There's one stumbling block here we should mention—the facilitation process has to be aimed at arriving at the solution to the root problem, not just conflict resolution. We're not looking for compromise, but for the best solution. That means everyone will not get their way. The team members must have enough faith in their leader that they'll defer their own preferences and implement the best solution.

• Additional characteristics of a good leader fall into the "other necessary skills" category, which include the willingness to persistently follow-up problems, the ability to speak the "language" of the various departments, the thorough understanding of the company's strategic goals and the like.

The Ideal Team

The team leader recruits the team from the company at large, with the members coming from all the company's departments. Some of the people are full-time, while others may be part-time. The people are brought on to the team as they are required and are freed up to go to other teams as soon as possible without compromising the development of the product.

> **Team members receive a performance review as they exit the team.**

The members, full-time or part-time, must be committed to the development of the product. To link the members to the effort, team members receive a performance review as they exit the team, regardless of the amount of time spent on the project. This review serves as a coaching and learning session as well as a performance appraisal. The salary and annual performance review is still handled by the functional department, but is heavily influenced by the team member's contribution to the success of the development effort.

Here's the truth of it—it's unlikely you'll get the ideal team structure. But you can come close.

The ideal product development team would have at least one full-time member from every discipline in the company. This is usually impossible. Consider Materials Planning or Finance. Each of these groups has a vital role to play in the development of the new product, but they both have factors that limit their representatives' full-time participation on the team. First, most companies have more than one new product under development at any given time. Unfortunately, in the real world, a company that has 15 new products under development can't afford 15 materials planners and 15 cost analysts working full-time on the projects. A second factor is that given modern computerized tools, materials planners and cost analysts can handle more than one project at a time. So the first step in assembling the product development methodology in regard to the team is how each department is going to participate.

Missing Functions?

It's possible to have a function that is not even represented by a part-time team member. That's usually the case with a manufacturing process expert for a process that is standardized and used by every product throughout the company. In our case, as an electronic company who assembles their own circuit boards, we extensively use wave soldering, but we only have a single wave soldering expert. While that person could be a part-time team member, there's another alternative. That person can participate in the MAP process either through classes for the full team or written specifications. This is an especially useful tool when you're dealing with experts from your suppliers, who may, in fact, be on the other side of the world. It's necessary for the process expert to be available for consultation in case the unforeseen rears its ugly head—so this can be considered participation by exception.

In addition, several individuals within a department might be needed to participate in the process. For example, a manufacturing engineering specialist on testing might need to be involved, since designing in the product testing procedures usually must begin on Day One. This specialist would be in addition to other representatives from manufacturing engineering.

At Bently Nevada, we have a "co-location desk" for specialists or other functional department members who may need to "sit in" with the team at various times. This is an actual desk, located with the new product development team and always ready for that visiting specialist. This provides for the necessity of having all functions being represented with the real-world confines of limited resources. Usually, the point at which we suggest a person move to the co-location desk is when the team's activities become a full-time job for that person.

The point is that we need to provide the best techniques for each situation. But exercise caution when deciding that a function doesn't need to have a member on the team. Too often, this omission is more a reflection of resource demands or simple oversight than for carefully considered reasons.

> We have a "co-location desk" for specialists or other functional department members who may need to "sit in" with the team.

Ideally, we want to create a situation where the departments themselves are insisting on participating in the process rather than waiting for an invitation—or a summons. One of the deadliest games impeding successful new product development is "Gotcha!" Or, "I knew that was a mistake, but nobody asked me." It is everyone's job to insist that the product be built right the first time! One of the ways of guaranteeing that is to not allow "Gotcha!" to develop.

A frequent criticism of involving all the departments in the process is that it makes the process longer. This is, of course, exactly the opposite of what we want to happen. We need to redirect the discussion away from suggesting the exclusion of a department to speed up the process to understanding what is actually slowing the process down. If we stick to the MAP process, we can sustain our speed improvements and still involve all the people who need to be involved.

Chapter 11

Toolkit: S-Curve

Deciding which new product to pursue and defining it in detail is more than just a difficult task—it's covered wagon time, serious pioneering work. We're all still feeling our way through the "Needs List," trying to select which idea is going to work; trying to get that much closer to our customers. Difficult indeed!

But difficult or not, it is critical that it be done right. To help us get it right, we can make use of some new MAP tools and techniques that improve and clarify the new product planning process. Among those tools, one of the most powerful is the S-Curve.

We are all familiar with the concept of product life-cycles. A new product is born, reaches its peak and then subsides, eventually dying off. We usually express this as a basic bell-shaped curve.

This view of a product's journey has been around for many years and has been written about and popularized by The Boston Consulting Group, Harvard Business School and others. The idea is that when a product is first introduced, its sales volume is low. As customers begin to accept the product, the sales volume increases. At some point, the product reaches its maximum sales volume, because the market saturates or a new product begins to supplant the original product. The sales volume then declines.

The curve may be steeper for more popular products, and it may be sharper for fad products. Commodity products tend to have broad curves with slow rates of changes in sales volumes that may go up and down cyclically. But, by and large, the product life-cycle curve is an accurate reflection of the life of a product.

What the life-cycle curve doesn't do, nor claim to do, is give us the information necessary to decide what our next new product should be. To tackle that task we need some additional tools, a second curve, the S-Curve.

Before we can talk about our second curve, we need to look at a concept introduced by Joel Arthur Barker in his book, *Future Edge*.

In order to help visualize his concept of paradigms, Barker suggested an S-shaped curve. When a new idea is proposed, it is slow to be used.

(At Point A on the chart).

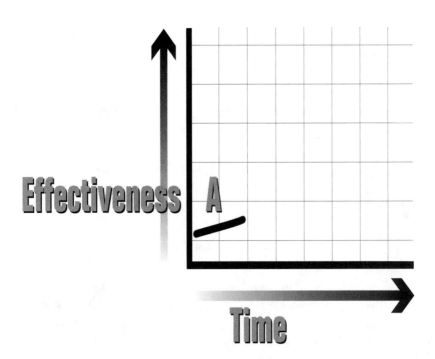

At first people don't understand or accept the new idea—or paradigm, so it's used to solve only a few problems. As more people begin to understand and accept the paradigm, the number of problems solved with its usage begins to increase. Success breeds success, more people accept the new way, and more problems are solved. The process is actually self-feeding as long as the paradigm is successful at solving the challenges at hand. This is Point B, where the line on the graph goes steadily upward.

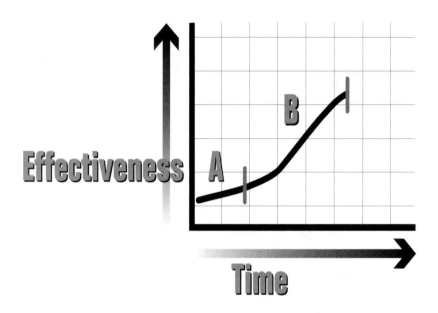

At some point (C, next page) the remaining problems become more difficult to solve with the new—now becoming the old—way, and the curve begins to flatten. Many problems still remain, but they are difficult or impossible to solve with the now popular paradigm. This second change in the line's slope, Barker contends, comes with the maturation of the paradigm, when it is running out of problems it can practically solve, resulting in the time-per-problem-solved becoming increasingly longer. At the top of the curve, Barker concludes, is when it is time to start thinking about shifting paradigms.

We can apply the concept of the paradigm S-Curve to new product development and arrive at a very useful tool, simply by

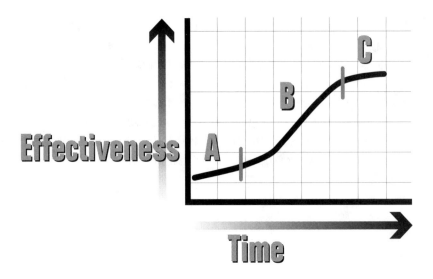

Effectiveness

Time

replacing the term paradigm with the term product architecture.

A product architecture is, in fact, a paradigm. Initially, it would take time for the new architecture to become accepted. Then, as our customers became more familiar with the concept, they would make better use of the product and more needs would be filled. Success again breeds success, and the number of problems being solved and needs being met would increase. Finally, the problems remaining for the customer would become difficult to solve with the new (now old) product architecture. Essentially, we have solved all the problems we can with that particular architecture, although the product itself continues on its product life-cycle curve for some time, solving the old problems.

The reason we emphasize architecture rather than product is that the journey up the S-Curve is frequently a series of products that represent an evolution of the architecture. A few features and functions of the first product offering were changed, evolving into the second product. The second product was made a little smaller, or less expensive, and evolved into the third product. And so on and so on. However, during the journey, the general product architecture remained the same and served the same marketplace.

A particular use of the S-Curve is very useful in product planning. We have to create our own S-Curve, with the X-axis being time and the Y-axis being problems solved or needs filled. The S-Curve quickly becomes a powerful tool to determine if the existing architecture should be evolved or an entirely new architecture should be developed. Viewed in this way, the S-Curve provides answers to some of our most vexing questions:

• Should our next product be an evolutionary step (same product architecture with additional features and functions), or do we need to go for a revolutionary step (a new product architecture), up to a new S-Curve?

• Which customers should you stay close to and when?

• When do the customers' verbalized wants and actual needs coincide?

• What is the timing of the likely revenue stream?

> A product architecture is, in fact, a paradigm.

• In what stage are the competition's products, and how do they relate to ours?

• What should be the detailed definition of the new product?

• Where are we at most risk from competitive products?

• What should we do if the competition has a successful new product idea?

Singles Or Home Runs?

It has become popular to call the evolution of existing architectures "singles." Singles refer to the fact that the evolution occurs in small steps, moving slowly up the S-Curve (Point B on the graph). When major changes are made and the product paradigm is shifted to an entirely new architecture (a new S-Curve), it is called a "home run."

Much to everyone's surprise, a recent R. D. Garwood roundtable on new product development pointed to the singles-home run question as a major challenge in new product planning. Although the consensus was that most companies try to hit too many home runs and not enough singles, no consensus existed on how to plan new products.

A company that pursues a singles strategy in new product development is true to the concept of continuous improvement, but puts itself at risk of losing to another company's home runs. On the other hand, a company that constantly goes for the home run will probably not survive the long haul, because of the high risk and costs associated with home runs.

Obviously, a World Class manufacturing company needs a strategy that balances singles and home runs. Singles represent a commitment to the customer, improvements to products the customer has already purchased. As one company told us, "We concentrate on singles, because we want to service our existing customer base. They expect us to be committed to our product line." Yet the occasional home run is essential to survive and thrive in the volatile, global market. If you don't create the replacement for your product architecture, someone else will.

> If you don't create the replacement for your product architecture, someone else will.

The MAP S-Curve can help us craft the balance between singles and home runs. Within the middle section of the curve, the customers are learning about the existing product and using it to solve more and more of their problems. As long as the product is solving most of the customers' new problems and all of the most important problems, it is appropriate to evolve the existing architecture. During this singles strategy, you are mainly determining which enhancements should be made to the existing product. Which features and functions should be added, deleted or modified? How can you improve the quality and reliability? How can the cost be reduced? How can the lead time be reduced?

Within the middle of the S-Curve, you want to stay close to the customers who are using your product. They understand the product paradigm and will be able to tell you how the product should evolve. As the customers use the products, they run into real life situations that indicate what should be done to improve their usefulness.

Tackling A Fishy Subject

If you were a maker of fishing tackle boxes, for example, it would be an excellent idea to stay close to people who fish. As fishermen (or women) used your products, they would discover, through real-life experiences, which lures wouldn't fit in the tackle drawers or whether the box tipped over too easily in a boat. Are the supplies conveniently organized, and is the tackle box the right size to conveniently fit into the trunk of a car or the back of a Jeep?

The customer understands the paradigm of the fishing tackle box and is able to express his or her needs in terms of the tackle box paradigm. The company that gathers this type of information and quickly incorporates it into the next evolutionary step in the product is the company that is going to be successful.

Keeping track of customer requests provides several important pieces of information. First, the requests tell you how to evolve—or enhance—your existing products. Second, you learn how many and which of the requests your existing product is unable to satisfy. Also, the unsatisfied requests can help you qualify which new concept will work when it comes time to shift the paradigm.

When the existing architecture begins to have difficulty solving customers' problems and fulfilling their needs (Point C on the graph), it's a signal that a different course of action is required. As a larger and larger percentage of the needs can not be fulfilled, you are approaching the top of the S-Curve, and a brand new product paradigm is required—you'll jump to the beginning of a new S-Curve. The rules for the product must be changed, so that it can deal with the outstanding issues. It's time to swing for the stands: a home run is in order.

Sticking with our tackle box example, maybe there's been a wholesale shift to fly fishing, and your company's tackle boxes are too big or unwieldy for the smaller flies.

It's surprising how often companies do not recognize that a product has reached the top of the S-Curve and a brand new idea is needed. Even when someone else comes up with the idea, our resistance to change keeps us from recognizing that our product badly needs to be replaced. Consider IBM and the personal computer wars.

> Our resistance to change keeps us from recognizing that our product badly needs to be replaced.

More than a decade ago, the personal computer began its trip up the S-Curve. At that time, IBM was deriving most of its revenue from the large margins on its mainframe computers. The mainframe computers were not only expensive, but they required significant investments in facilities with false floors, air conditioning and computer operations staffs. IBM customers realized the computer was a key to productivity improvements and modern business practices. But all too often, the investment was high and the application was difficult to support. Many of the applications were too expensive and couldn't be justified by the return. The customer's need for low-cost computing power was not being fulfilled.

Other companies, most notably Apple, were pioneering the new product paradigm, the personal computer. The cost of computing power was significantly less, and the PC did not require special facilities or staffs. Even as companies began to use PCs and third-party software to fulfill word processing needs, IBM did not acknowledge the precarious position of the mainframe business.

Industry observers believe IBM's reluctance to acknowledge the situation stemmed from the threat the PC represented to their core business. IBM had built an organization that was staffed and funded with the large margins on mainframe sales. The concern for lost revenue to pay for the world's best service organization was overwhelming.

IBM's first response—or tactic—was to dismiss the PC as a toy that would never be able to handle corporate business or infiltrate the corporate market. But when Apple began to gain a significant market share for the PC, IBM assembled a small staff to try to quickly develop an IBM PC. All the while, IBM was spending the majority of its time trying to protect mainframe sales.

The focus on the threat to mainframe sales was blinding the company to the new opportunities with the new product paradigm.

Engrossed in mainframe issues, IBM decided to subcontract the PC operating system to Bill Gates Jr., and Microsoft was born. Companies like Word Perfect, Lotus and Autodesk were allowed—even encouraged—to provide the application software for word processing, spread sheets and computer-aided drafting.

Much of the revenue in the computer business was shifting from hardware to software. If IBM had decided it would travel up the PC S-Curve faster than other companies, billions of dollars in software revenue could have softened the revenue decreases in mainframe business. Many of us now think IBM didn't see that opportunity because it didn't realize the mainframe business was at the top of the S-Curve. The company devoted much of its time and resources to protect a product that was not fulfilling many of the customer's needs, while someone else was building on the PC home run with software singles.

Good Old Hindsight

It is always easy, with 20/20 hindsight, to see someone else's business problems and mistakes. Why is it so difficult to bring the same objectivity to our own business situations? In our own business situations, the threats and challenges are real and will affect our livelihood. And when your job is threatened, it's much more difficult to be objective. Nonetheless, situations will come up where a home run is in order. We need to recognize this point— and react accordingly and in a timely manner.

At the top of the curve, we need to stay close to a totally different customer—the "outsider." The rules of the product must be changed totally, not just modified slightly. It is very difficult for people who have a vested interest in a product to clearly see that new architecture is required. While there are exceptions, most of us are so accustomed to thinking in terms of the current product that we have a difficult time with the breakthrough thinking required. Others have a more specific vested interest, such as sales commission, and do not want things to change.

As Joel Barker points out, it is generally going to be an outsider that is going to make the breakthrough and devise the new way—the new paradigm, the new product.

> You must stay focused on the customer needs—not your own; nor what your company "does best."

This is even more difficult, because the outsider may be actually hostile to our existing products and may have reluctantly bought them—because there was "nothing better out there." But at the top of the S-Curve, we must stay close to innovators without that vested interest in the existing products.

Not all of the outside ideas will actually fulfill the customer's needs. At this point, you gather, summarize and evaluate each of the new architectures that has been suggested by outsiders and insiders. Key to the initial evaluation is to compare the list of needs the existing product could not satisfy to the new suggestions to determine which of the new ideas is most likely to succeed.

This is not an easy process and is sometimes based more on intuition—gut instinct—than desired for sound business practice. You must remain open-minded, or you may find yourself rationalizing that all the changes are bad. You must stay focused on the customer needs—not your own; nor what your company "does best"—if you are going to see clearly the next successful product. The home run is difficult because it represents change—and all the risk that comes with change.

Revenue Timing

It is dangerous to talk about degrees in paradigm shifts, because many people think that a natural evolution of an existing paradigm is actually a new paradigm. At the point almost all of the product "rules" have changed, however, is the point you are involved with a new product paradigm.

New product paradigms are difficult to sell. Getting people to accept innovation requires hurdling many obstacles. The resistance stems from the belief that a new paradigm is going to take more time to become accepted, and, therefore, the revenue will be slower in coming. You are starting at the bottom of the S-Curve and will not start generating significant revenue until the product reaches the middle of the curve. With a minor modification of an existing product, the revenues should start flowing more quickly.

Management consultant and communications expert Jim R. Bright identified a number of tactics aimed at helping us move to the middle of the curve faster. The questions directing the tactics include:

• Have you been able to show the user the perceived advantage of the new product? In other words, does the user really understand that the new product will solve the user's problem?

• Have you simplified, or facilitated, the user's understanding of the innovation?

• Have you developed a trust relationship with the user?

We often think that all new products should generate revenue very quickly. When working with new product paradigms, the revenue streams will take longer to be realized, so, when planning, we need to take into account how well prepared we are to overcome the obstacles to innovation.

Making Money Versus Spending Money

The S-Curve illustrates some very powerful business strategies. During the beginning of the curve, very few people use the new idea—or product—to fill their needs and solve their problems. The idea is being taught to reluctant students by the entrepreneur and a few brave pioneers. Training programs must be developed to overcome people's resistance to the new concept. These training programs should address people inside the organization as well as outside.

Regulatory organizations must be convinced the new idea is safe and compatible with the organization's objectives. Extensive testing often is required to assure these entities that it is acceptable to go forward. When a pharmaceutical company develops a new drug to combat a disease, it is not sufficient that the drug actually be a successful cure. The FDA must be convinced the drug is safe and adheres to government regulations and guidelines. Most of the time, the cost of this approval effort dwarfs the discovery and refinement cost.

The new idea frequently needs to be supported by new processes that also must be developed. This process is usually expensive and time-consuming. The new processes are necessary not only in manufacturing, but also in any number of other areas. For example, the new product often addresses the needs of a different customer, and the sales force needs to become familiar with this new customer. Often the product will require different service techniques than its predecessor, and entirely new service plans will need to be developed.

> This part of the S-Curve is called the spend money part of the curve for obvious reasons.

While the resources—money, time, energy—are being expended at a rapid rate, the new product is neither well-known nor well-accepted. Its usage is not widespread, and the sales volume is small. Very little revenue is being generated to offset the costs that are being incurred. This part of the S-Curve is called the spend money part of the curve for obvious reasons—you are spending more money than you are making.

Some new products never exit this stage. Sometimes, the new product paradigm doesn't fill the customer's need. Other times, the regulatory agencies may not approve the product and it doesn't get the chance to fill the need. And sometimes we simply fail to overcome the customer's resistance to innovation. Under any one of these circumstances, our efforts have resulted only in the expenditure of money and resources; significant revenue will not be generated to carry on the business cycle.

It is very risky to try for home runs only. Many of the "swing for the fence" efforts will end as they do in baseball—three strikes and you're out. There are many hurdles to overcome in successfully introducing totally new innovations, and the results associated with such ideas are uncertain.

But home runs, as any Sunday afternoon fan knows, are not impossible. Some of the new paradigms will be accepted, learned and enhanced. The more the needs are fulfilled, the more the paradigm is accepted. Product reliability increases, product cost is reduced and selected features and functions are added to the product as enhancements. The acceptance of the concept becomes more widespread, and the sales volume increases. During this part of the ride up the curve, the product is in the make money mode. The sales revenues exceed the expenditure rates, and the business cycle is sustained.

Spend Or Make?

The division of the S-Curve into a spend money area and a make money area has some very interesting ramifications—no, make that life or death implications—for business tactics. It is essentially a middle-of-the-curve strategy that is used by re-source-strapped companies to build successful enterprises. When resources are scarce, using critical time and money to research hit-or-miss new product ideas is risky business. The most successful strategy is to look around for new product ideas that have already passed through the expensive and risky pioneer phase on the S-Curve, are already being accepted and are already solving the customer's problems. You can then use your critical resources to progress up the S-Curve ahead of the other companies. This is usually achieved by adding features and functions, improving the quality and reliability and reducing the cost.

The Japanese didn't invent automobiles, steel or many of the other product paradigms that make them successful. But they did excel at taking these products up the S-Curve by improving reliability, reducing cost and enhancing features and functions faster than the competition. It is important to note that you cannot move up the S-Curve by simply copying the competition's product. You must understand the paradigm the product represents, and you must understand the customer's needs so that you can accurately enhance the product.

If you did create the new product paradigm, you must work

hard to get up the S-Curve ahead of all the other people who will be tempted to get on the S-Curve with you. If you didn't create the new product paradigm, you must work hard to prove that you can better the pioneers of the concept. There are several advantages to this approach.

> Evolving an existing product architecture is less risky than the creation of an entirely new product.

Evolving an existing product architecture is less risky than the creation of an entirely new product. It is easier to get marketing data because the customers already understand and are "conversant" in the product paradigm. The learning curve for people is shorter. The development steps are smaller and the technical risks are more manageable. And, resistance to small steps is much less than what is experienced with the giant leap taken by completely new products.

A primary benefit of this business strategy—i.e., enhancing, not creating—is that all your activity takes place during the make money part of the curve. Sales volumes are already high because similar products are already being used to fill the customer's needs. The revenue stream can be used to support the product as it progresses. Many people believe this is precisely the strategy that Japan used to get its industry off the ground after World War II.

On the other hand, innovative companies like Hewlett Packard have such an intuitive understanding of their customers for their low-cost printers that they are able to consistently jump from S-Curve to S-Curve, shifting easily from singles to home runs before their competition has a chance.

What If The Competition Has It First?

Often, we find ourselves in the undesirable position of being beat to the punch by the competition, who developed a new product concept before you may even have thought of it. When this occurs, take some basic steps to remedy the situation.

You need to try to "objectively" determine whether the competition's new idea is solving problems your products are not.

It is extremely difficult to be objective in these circumstances, but objectivity is essential to develop the most effective course of action. If the competition's new product is solving important problems, you must respond. If you don't, you can lose that portion of the marketplace.

However, it is self-defeating to chase the competition's features and functions. You will always be one step behind. Once the competition has established a new paradigm, which is becoming accepted because it is fulfilling needs, the only successful strategies are to develop a more successful paradigm or to go up the S-Curve faster than the competitor, not slower.

In either case, you want to try to understand the paradigm itself, not the features and functions. You need to understand the problems the product is solving that your product is not. You need to understand the new product rules and figure out how to evolve them faster than the competition or find a new rule set that is even better at fulfilling the needs.

Do Needs Equal Wants?

The question "Should we go for a single or a home run?" is closely related to the question "When do the customers' spoken wants equal their actual needs?" Every company hears from its customers what they want, but just as not all internal suggestions should be implemented automatically, not all customer suggestions are worth development or enhancement of a product.

Tom Peters is right: we need to be close to our customers.

But which customers, and when?

The S-Curve concept helps answer these questions. In the middle of the curve, most of the customers understand the products and how to apply them. These customers are gaining experience with the product every day. As they apply the product, they empirically learn what improvements should be made. Empirical learning is very effective, and there is a strong likelihood the customers' ideas will accurately reflect the true situation, hence their actual needs.

In addition, communication will be particularly effective

under these circumstances. There is a common rule set to communicate with—the product itself. So, during the middle of the S-Curve, we want to listen to the customers who understand the product and are using it. Their spoken wants will have a strong correlation to their needs.

> **We need to be listening to people who do not have a vested interest in the existing product.**

The story is different when we get to the top of the curve. At the top of the curve, we need an entirely new product architecture. We need to be listening to people who do not have a vested interest in the existing product. Often, these are the people we don't particularly like because they didn't sign up for the old product. They were critical of our approach.

However, since these people don't have a vested interest in the old product, they are more likely to do the breakthrough thinking necessary to come up with the completely new idea.

So at the top of the curve, when we've decided it's time for a home run, we listen to people who may not be using our products. They may not even be customers. And we almost surely won't like them, because they are outsiders—i.e., outside our way of thinking. If this breakthrough thinker is an insider, the other people in the company will be asking, "What in world is he/she doing now?" These are the times that an entrepreneur steps in and fills a need the customer may not even recognize.

Chapter 12

Toolkit: Measurements

Whenever we go on a journey, it helps to plan certain activities to guarantee the journey's success. If planning a wilderness hike, for example, a map helps to chart the plan and might include the location of the trailhead from which we'll begin, noting which landmarks we'll pass, and determining where we'll finish the hike. During the hike, we'll use the map and compass to keep us on course. If we peak a certain ridge expecting to see a lake, but—surprise—no body of water beckons us onward, it's time to take a break and see what went wrong. Are we off course? Is the map wrong? Did the lake dry up?

The key point is that we must resolve the issue of what happened to the lake—before we continue our journey forward. If we discover that, in fact, we scaled the wrong ridge, then we need to determine where we actually are and develop an alternative plan to get us to the final objective.

In our new product development process, we need to follow the same methodology—a series of pre-determined landmarks to tell us whether or not we're on course. We need landmarks—

measurements—for the quality of the product, the quality of the process, the timeliness of the project, the timeliness of the process, the cost of the project, the cost of the product and the overall effectiveness of the product and, of course, the process.

Typically, under the old paradigm, the only measurements are whether the new product development project is completed on time and within budget. Those measurements, ironically, can work against us. For example, a project completed on time and under budget, but with significant product quality problems, doesn't serve us very well—we have quickly and efficiently arrived at a place off the map. Secondly, note the linkage between product and process. If we do not set landmarks for both, we will face a constant element of uncertainty as to where we are and where we're going.

As we put our measurements in place, it's important to realize that the absolute number for many of these measurements may not be known, and often trying to set an absolute goal can result in a lot of nonproductive discussion about what is an "attainable number." The best way to handle this situation is to establish the current baseline performance, then expect that the situation will be improved. Better, or, at least, faster, to arrive in sight of our lake—a little closer each time—than to spend months establishing the exact longitude and latitude we must hit in order to say we've arrived. Potential landmarks for the new product development journey include product quality, timeliness, costs and overall process effectiveness. Let's review each in detail.

Product Quality

As we discussed, effective measurement of a new product is often a major challenge. In the first place, the actual quality of the product under user's conditions isn't known until it's been in the marketplace for a period of time. This time lag between the cause of the problem (whether defined, designed or manufactured in) and its discovery (during usage) creates a sort of psychic time lag for the product development team—"All that happened a long time ago; I'm already on another project..."

Second, there's a ripple effect created by measurements, often resulting in undesirable side effects. For example, the number of changes that must be made after a product is in the marketplace is a good indicator of how well the product was planned and designed. However, if we announce our plan to track the number of changes, we run the risk that people might avoid making necessary changes to keep the change number low— "Don't make the change, and it won't show up as a problem in the measurements."

The best way to minimize this problem is to keep the emphasis on measuring the process rather than individual performance. This approach is appropriate, because, in most cases, the problem is with the process, not an individual. When the measurements are used as a participatory tool to improve the business and are not a threat to any individual, less game playing will occur. But beware, it takes just a couple of inadvertent finger pointing on the manager's part to collapse the whole process.

> Keep the emphasis on measuring the process rather than individual performance.

During the Design Phase, the products are tested to verify their performance. This first line of quality measurement provides an opportunity for problem discovery and initiates corrective action. The main focus is to not release the product to manufacturing until it performs as expected. This area has been covered extensively in recent years, and few of us will debate the need to test and verify a product's performance. While product testing measures the quality of the design process, it is not an adequate indicator of the product definition. Most often, product definition problems only become apparent after the product is in the marketplace.

Measuring quality after a product is in the marketplace gives you an evaluation the progress of the definition and design methods. The amount of money that must be spent on corrections or enhancements to a product after it is in the marketplace (say, warranty claims) is a good indicator of product quality. The more money (or other resources) that must be spent after release, the poorer the quality. This has the added advantage, as quality pioneer Phil Crosby stressed in his landmark book *Quality Is Free*, of being expressed in financial terms—dollars and cents have a way of getting people's attention.

Marketplace activity must be taken into account when measuring progress and comparing performance on many different projects. Products experiencing heavy usage in the market generate more requests for changes, improvements or defect corrections. Measuring the ratio of the sustaining cost—that is, any cost incurred during or after the Launch Phase—to the revenue generated takes marketplace activity into account.

The sustaining costs measurement is also a good indicator of whether a product has been prematurely released to manufacturing and design activity is actually continuing under the guise of sustaining the product—something that happens all too often.

If the accounting system is unable to measure the sustaining cost of a product and compare it to actual revenues, another approach is to measure the number of changes that must be made after the product is released. This approach is not as accurate, because it doesn't differentiate between large and small changes. As with sustaining measurements, it is better to ratio the measurement with the revenue generated to factor in marketplace activity.

Timeliness

We all understand dates, and deadlines are the easiest dates of all to grasp, which is why timeliness measurements—deadlines—are put in place so quickly.

Because a deadline is a fixed, concrete, measurable point, more emphasis is placed on the due dates than often is intended. People may disagree or be uncertain about quality measurements, but they know very well when they overrun the deadline. As a result, they will default to the measurement they most clearly understand. Quality takes a back seat to timeliness.

To keep timeliness from being the overriding measurement, product managers and project leaders must constantly monitor a most important communications tool—their own actions. If, for example, product testing is not going very well, but the leader's actions are all aimed at hitting the deadline, the quality priority will be sacrificed. If, instead, the leader insists that the project be done correctly, despite an underlying sense of urgency, the priorities will be kept straight.

A second undesirable consequence of a timeliness focus is padding schedules. If individual success is strongly tied to making the date, people will often add a little time here and there, because they know something will indeed go wrong. The problem, of course, with padded schedules is that they are self-fulfilling prophecies. The emphasis must be on aggressive schedules to keep the product development cycle short. Even if the project runs a little over the estimated times, but the development time was competitive, the effort should be considered a success.

> The emphasis must be on aggressive schedules to keep the product development cycle short.

We shouldn't have to say this, but we still do. If the project falls behind schedule, it's necessary to readjust the schedule so the efforts of the entire company are well coordinated. As we move toward making new product development a company-wide effort, this communication function becomes even more critical.

Two facets of timeliness are incorporated into the development of new products: individual product development projects must be measured, and the timeliness of the overall product development process must be accessed. To successfully reach the timeliness landmarks, you must be able to correctly estimate (plan the trip), and you must be able to control the time it will take to make the journey. Individual projects are typically managed with PERT (Program Evaluation and Review Technique) or CPM (Critical Path Method) tools. Either of these methods proves effective in controlling projects. Definition and design completion dates are important milestones, which can be used by the entire company to evaluate individual projects.

Unlike the measurement of timeliness within individual

projects, measuring the timeliness of the entire MAP process is not widely practiced for the simple reason that it's more difficult to do. But the benefits are tremendous. Even with today's focus on faster cycle times, many companies actually don't know how long their cycle times run or whether they are getting longer or shorter.

The elapsed times required to define and design a product are the key indicators.

The measurement is the average elapsed time for all new products developed in the last year (13 four-week periods). If the average time frame is longer than one year, the effect of the improvements is averaged out and the time lag between improvements and measured results becomes too long. If some averaging is not done, the measurement is too erratic, and it is difficult to detect trends.

Costs

The variety and latitude of cost collection methods can make the measure of costs difficult. Even under generally accepted accounting principles (GAAP), the techniques of gathering costs and where that cost is accumulated vary greatly. GAAPs have been developed to ensure uniform understanding of financial reports, focused on reporting to people external to the company and to governmental agencies. The financial reporting required to support product development is somewhat different than GAAP, and the system must be designed accordingly. Product development costs, sustaining costs and generated revenue are three cost measurements of interest and should be available from accounting systems without excessive effort.

Product Development Costs

Product development cost is estimated during the Definition Phase, and is used to decide what the financial ramifications of a project might be, thus allowing us to move to the Design Phase. Generally, if the estimated revenues exceed the development cost estimate by a certain ratio, the project is considered a good financial investment. Product development cost is presented to the PDRB as a lump sum, but the project leader has product development cost as time-phased and with incremental task data. This enables the project leader to use the financial data as a management tool to find and correct problems during the Design Phase.

Even after the project has been released, some engineering expenditures usually occur on the project. Often, these are handled as sustaining expenses rather than R&D expenses from an accounting point of view. It is important for these expenditures to be attributed to the product development cost measurements. This is especially important in sensitive cases where a product has been released before the design is actually completed. It's far too easy to "bury" the actual cost, feeding us false information on which we will then make future decisions.

Revenue

The amount of revenue a product will generate is also estimated during the Definition Phase. After the product is introduced to the marketplace, the actual revenues are compared to the estimates. The accuracy of those predictions is a good measure of how well we understand the marketplace and how effective our Launch Phase has been. Revenue is tracked for as long as the product is considered a "new" product—usually five years for industrial products; three years for more volatile consumer products. The feedback provided by this process provides a "conscience" for the process of deciding how to use the product development resources, ideally keeping us from relying on the jump-to-conclusion style of allocating the resources.

Another way to look at revenue measurements is the ratio between the revenue and the development cost. This provides an idea of the return on investments that a particular product yields. Your company should have an idea of the return necessary to consider a project successful.

Product Cost

Product cost has become more critical in recent years as more and more competitors pour into the marketplace. The result of the influx of competitors is that customers now have a better educated idea of what they're willing to pay for a specific product. The price the customer is willing to pay becomes the driver for the cost at which the product must be manufactured if the desired margins are going to be achieved. For new products to be considered a financial success, the manufacturing cost must be low enough to provide an acceptable margin.

Both the sales price and the manufacturing costs influence the margin that the product contributes to the enterprise. Each of these should be measured separately so, if problems arise, it will be easier to trace the root causes. During the Definition Phase, both sales price and manufacturing costs are estimated—usually time-phased estimates based on the amount of time the product is in the marketplace. These estimates become landmarks to determine if everything is going according to plan as the product begins generating revenue. If there are problems, the respective departments (Manufacturing and Sales) should handle those problems.

Effectiveness Of The Overall MAP Process

Since the fundamental purpose of developing a new product is to generate revenue, the overall effectiveness of the product development process is measured in financial terms. Two measurements involving revenues give a good indication of how well the product development process is going. First, the total revenue generated by all current new products compared to the total development cost of those projects indicates the average effectiveness of the process. Making the measurement a ratio helps establish a baseline as the company grows.

The second indicator of the health of the process is to measure the percentage of current sales derived from new products. This gives a good indication as to how well the company is updating its product lines. In the case of this measurement, there is an optimum point for any company. If the percentage of sales stemming from new products is too low, the product lines are not being updated often enough, which could give your competitor an opening. If the percentage is too high, the sales people—and the customers—are in a constant churn, always needing to learn new products. This percentage, though, varies from industry to industry and with each individual company's strategy.

> The overall effectiveness of the product development process is measured in financial terms.

New product development is a process. As with any process, we judge its effectiveness by whether it conforms to expectations. We need to develop the expectations for the new product development process, then put in place the measurements to gauge whether we're meeting those expectations.

Chapter 13

Toolkit:
Cost Management

Managing costs in new product development consists of two specific issues. Too often, however, the costs are treated as a single issue.

The first is management of the cost to develop the product; the second is management of the cost to manufacture the product. What has characteristically been the case is that the cost of making the product receives short shrift during the development, with many companies paying more attention to the development cost than the product cost until the product is being manufactured.

The New Product Cost Paradigm

In the old cost paradigm, we developed the product, calculated the cost, marked it up and sold it. The shift, though, is now from "cost-driving-price" (CDP) to "price-driving-costs" (PDC). To illustrate, let's think about bicycles. In the old days of not-so-many years ago, we all rode heavy cruiser bicycles, fire-engine red. When a bicycle company wanted to build a new model, it put its engineers on alert. The engineers wrote up the specs, added estimated prices for each component, then passed the list on to management. Management added up the component cost, tacked on an appropriate profit margin, then announced that the new 1956 Super Cruiser Deluxe bike would be available the next year for $36, up from the previous year's $29. When the bike was actually delivered, the cost was $38.27, plus tax, and your dad and mom just shook their heads.

Notice several things about this process:

• Annual cost increases were assumed, not only by management, but by the customers as well.

• The thrust for product costing came from Engineering.

• Controls on component costs were minimal. If there were cost overruns, they were passed on to the customer.

The world of that fire-engine red cruiser is dead and gone. Annual cost increases are no longer assumed—just the opposite is true. Top mountain bike producers, for example, now race to bring the newest, most expensive race-driven technological developments to low-end bikes. It only took a couple of years, for example, for motorcycle-type suspension to migrate from $4,000 race bikes to $500 entry-level bikes.

Bicycle companies aren't the only manufacturers feeling the more-for-less pinch. Look at the personal computer industry. Every new generation of personal computer offers faster, bigger, more powerful—for less money. One of the classic success stories of this frenetic industry is the Hewlett Packard laser printer series. Each new generation of the HP laser printer offers better print quality, faster printing, more useful features—and a lower price tag.

How can that be?

The answer is intelligent product cost management during the new product development process.

The first step is shifting from "cost-driving-price" to "price-driving-cost."

In "price-driving-cost," the first key factor to establish is what the market will pay for the product.

That sounds pretty obvious, doesn't it? Well then, why don't we take that step? Because it's harder than it seems at first. For the PDC method to work, it's got to be at the very root of the process.

Let's go back to our bicycle. Say we have a bicycle company, and we've decided to enter the hotly competitive mountain bike market. We do our market research, and we realize that the customers are hungry for bikes in the $750 range. We might sell such a bike to our dealers for $500, and we want to make $200 margin on each bike. That leaves us a $300 target cost to shoot for.

Defining Our Bike

We now need to define the product, keeping in mind the $300 target cost to us. The first thing we need to do is break the bike down into pieces—frame, wheels and tires, front fork, gears, small parts. Before we expend any new product development resources at all, we need to sit down at a table and make our "rule-of-thumb" estimate on what each of those subassemblies will cost. That rule-of-thumb doesn't just come out of the air, either. We know that last time the frame cost us $175, but we've got some new technology in place that should offer us some savings. There's been a reduction in the cost of the metal tubing as well, so the "guess" is—must be—rooted in reality.

Bicycle: Target Price: $500 Target Cost: $300	
Major Product Elements	Initial $ Estimate: Definition Phase
Wheels	60
Gears	50
Frame	150
Front Fork	40
Other	50
Total	$350

We discover that our rule-of-thumb estimates are $150 for the frame, $50 for the gears, $40 for the front forks, $60 for the wheels and tires and $50 in small parts. We add these prices, and we see a $350 bicycle.

Before we've had the first design meeting, we already realize we're going to have to remove $50 from the cost of manufacturing the bike to hit our price point. We purchase the gears and wheels, so we might be able to carve $10-15 out of that by smart shopping. We assemble the front forks, so there might be some flex there. But we plan to design and build the frame from scratch, and we need to remove one-third of the cost of building that frame.

Bicycle:	Target Price: $500	Target Cost: $300
Major Product Elements	Initial $ Estimate: Definition Phase	Revised $ Estimate: Definition Phase
Wheels	60	50
Gears	50	40
Frame	150	120
Front Fork	40	40
Other	50	50
Total	$350	$300

Before we take another step, we need to know whether we can meet that $120 cost for the frame.

Because, if we can't, it's time to stop the project! If we continue, several things can happen. The frame is a critical component. All the other bicycle components are designed to fit the frame. If we proceed without knowing whether we can meet the frame cost, we are locking ourselves into the design regardless of what the frame costs. For example, if we change the frame after designing the handle bars and stem, we will have to change the handlebar/stem assembly as well. The gearing is specified for the original frame design. If we have to modify that design later down the line, we'll also have to change the gearing. Suddenly, it's too expensive to redesign the frame to use less expensive production methods. We're trapped with the more expensive frame.

Product Love Affairs

It's easy to fall in love with a new product. Too often, what happens at this point is we press on into the design stage, trusting that we'll make up the $50 somewhere. We might assume we'll use lower-priced steel for the frame instead of aluminum; we might assume we'll acquire a new welding technology that will allow us to reduce the labor in the frame. We table the cost question, and start designing. About midway through the Design Phase, we discover the lower-priced steel doesn't deliver the structural rigidity we need for all the components to function correctly, so we go back to the higher-priced aluminum. Or we discover the new welding technology is not without its bugs, so we have to "dance" a little. Besides, the rationale goes, we're so far into the project, it makes more sense to go forward.

No. It makes more sense to design the frame first. We create an estimated bill of material for the frame subassembly and roll up those costs. We look at the processes we're using for manufacturing the frame and search for possible savings in those processes. Remember, we are still in the rule-of-thumb estimate stage here. We have not committed large amounts of time and money to product design. Once we are secure that we can, in fact, build a frame for $120, we need to look just as closely at each other subassembly. Maybe we should consider building our own front fork, which we estimate will cost us $35 each. What will it cost us in both time and money to set up our manufacturing line for such forks? Can we be assured that we can deliver a high-quality item for that price? Maybe we have some existing technology that we can make use of. Notice that even at the earliest stages, it's necessary for new product development to be a company-wide project. Manufacturing might know of process streamlining that can have a direct affect on making the frame. Purchasing might have heard of some competitive pricing on gears from another supplier. Engineering might be researching some esoteric materials that have application to frame manufacturing.

The reason we spend so much time on the cost estimates up front is that we're going to do something really wild and crazy— we're going to write those estimates down, and the team is going to continually refer to them as we move into a more solid cost estimate.

In our example, the calculated cost has risen to $310 because of increased fork costs and other small parts. At this point, we must make a decision on whether to proceed or shut down the project. For an additional $10, we'd probably continue.

It's probably safe to say that everybody makes some kind of cost estimates. Engineers' desks are full of them, usually stuffed into the back corners of desk drawers. What we want to do is set up a mechanism where, as we move into the Design Phase, the actual costs, rolled up from initial bills of material and routings, are compared back to the estimates, and the differences reconciled.

Bicycle: Target Price: $500 Target Cost: $300			
Major Product Elements	**Initial $ Estimate: Definition Phase**	**Revised Estimate: Definition Phase**	**Calculated Cost: Design Phase**
Wheels	60	50	45
Gears	50	40	40
Frame	150	120	125
Front Fork	40	40	45
Other	50	50	55
Total	**$350**	**$300**	**$310**

When we begin the design after the definition, we should design the items with the most significant cost risks first. In our bicycle company, we begin designing the frame. We contact aluminum companies for actual estimates, we get precise measurements of the welding and assembly times, all the minutiae that contribute to the actual costs. From these, we create the "calculated estimate." We still don't have the final cost of the product, but we're moving from our "rule-of-thumb" to a more solid measurement. Once we have the calculated estimate, we meet to compare that estimate with the rule-of-thumb. The primary question we hope to answer is whether we're still on target for our costs. We also want to constantly monitor the design of our highest risk, as well as highest cost, subassemblies. A bicycle frame, for example, is a critical part. Not only does it have to meet our cost estimates, but it has to be sufficiently strong to survive, provide the customer with an excellent ride—a hard thing to define—and enable all the other parts to fit correctly. The finest wheels, forks and gears in the world mean little if the frame snaps under use. Since critical parts affect many other parts, trouble

Bicycle:	Target Price: $500	Target Cost: $300		
Major Product Elements	Initial $ Estimate: Definition Phase	Revised Estimate: Definition Phase	Calculated Cost: Design Phase	Actual Cost: Launch Phase
Wheels	60	50	45	47
Gears	50	40	40	38
Frame	150	120	125	122
Front Fork	40	40	45	43
Other	50	50	55	55
Total	$350	$300	$310	$305

areas must be addressed immediately. Otherwise, a high-cost critical part tends to get frozen into the design as the other parts are completed. We design and decide to manufacture a set of forks, for example, which are perfectly tuned for a stiff aluminum frame. Midway through the design process, we find that there's no way we can hit our price point with an aluminum frame. But we've just spent X dollars tooling up for the special fork...

As we move through the process, costs solidify.

Purchase orders and work orders give us the actual costs, which are compared to the previous stage of estimates. The key point is that you must put into place a cost management system that constantly compares each successive estimate to the previous estimate and then asks, "Why?" In our bicycle case, the actual cost comes to $305, close to our revised Definition Phase estimate. If the newest estimate doesn't bear the slightest relationship to the previous estimate, we've got to know what went wrong, not only for this project, but for future projects as well.

Avoiding The Pitfalls

Product costs management processes face four common pitfalls:

1) "Yeah, sure—we can do it at that price..." The sales people representing suppliers, being an optimistic lot, will aggressively estimate prices to get their product designed into your product. Part of the profile of a successful salesperson is optimism, and sometimes that optimism gets translated into low-balling initial prices. However, as reality sets in and production gets closer and closer, the pricing has a tendency to increase.

> We should design the items with the most significant cost risks first.

In some companies, this price creep isn't even noticed, since Engineering obtained the pre-production estimates and Purchasing later asks for the quotes to build the product in quantity. The two quotes were different, but there was no mechanism to compare the quotes or manage the situation.

As they say in the movies, albeit old ones, "What we have here is a failure to communicate." On several levels. Had the suppliers been part of the process early on, they'd know that each new estimate is compared to the previous estimate, and there's less inclination to low-ball either by intent or ignorance. When Purchasing and Engineering are both represented on the product development team, clear comparisons can be made between earlier pre-production estimates and larger quantity orders.

2) Product volume is often a source of confusion in product cost management. Often, when engineers estimate costs, they use

the high volume numbers the product will eventually achieve. "Our engineers get better prices than we can," says Purchasing. In the first blush of optimism, those big volume prices look good. And, second, we might make "minor" changes in the components without going back to refigure the estimated costs. But production starts out at lower numbers, and the costs can be higher than expected, because suppliers may charge more for lower volumes. Solution? Establish volume expectations and associated cost changes up front. Write them down and track them.

3) The tendency in the early, more fluid days of product definition is to not break up the initial estimates in a manner that leads to easy cost comparisons as the product is designed. The initial estimates should be made on units that are likely to be a bill of material unit when the product is actually built. It's much easier to track evolving costs, for example, of the frame and the fork as opposed to a frame/fork assembly. If we lumped the frame and fork together and estimated the whole thing at $300, we might not catch the cost problems with the frame until it was too late (or too expensive) to make changes.

4) The biggest, most dangerous pitfall of all is simply to not systematically look at the cost of a new product as it is developed. The original estimate is made, then set aside until the project is done. Then we haul out the estimate and try to figure out what happened. Yes, new product development is an enormously

Evolution of Product Costs

Phase	Cost Method
Definition	Rule–of–thumb estimate
	↓
Definition	Revised estimate
	↓
Design	Bill of material roll up
	↓
Launch	Actual

complex task with many activities demanding immediate attention. But that doesn't mean that the cost issue can be defaulted. Cost problems must be caught early enough to correct them.

Product costs move through a specific evolution, from a rule of thumb estimate to actual costs. The key is to constantly monitor the estimate versus actual costs, then reconcile the differences.

Development Cost

The management of new product development projects is exactly the same as any other project management.

> The key is to constantly monitor the estimate versus actual costs, then reconcile the differences.

Real-time feedback of costs as the project proceeds and the reconciliation of differences between actual and estimates is a powerful learning tool. The sad truth is that too many companies focus on only the current project and why the estimates were not more accurate—in other words, fixing blame rather than using the experience as a learning opportunity to improve the overall process. Management does need to be demanding on some issues, and in the rare case when an individual is negligent or just not able to perform, some action must be taken. But far more new product development team leaders have been taken out and shot, figuratively, of course, than is necessary.

Note two important points about project costing: the first is that our ability to estimate gets better with practice. The second is that the most common reason for development cost overruns is stretching out the time of the project. The better product definition we have, the less likely we are to have the project stretch out.

Chapter 14

Final Exam:
Are We Guaranteed
Success?

For the last two decades, many businesses have been in upheaval. We've had to address major issues in quality, in our business processes, in our response time, in the global market. We've TQM'ed, empowered, just-in-timed, re-engineered and on and on. After all that work, it's time for the final exam.

Our ability to develop new products is that final exam.

We have moved from the age of mass production to a form of mass individualism—like the burger commercial says, the customers want it their way. And they will get it their way—either from us or from our competitors!

Without a consistent way to deliver a continuous flow of new products to the market, it doesn't matter how evolved our business processes are. We run the risk of becoming an agile, low-cost provider of just-in-time, zero-defect, ecologically correct, obsolete products.

Product life-cycles aren't getting any longer; the cost of

development isn't insignificant—and that money is just as "green" as any other cost that erodes profit.

We must increase our "batting average" on new product successes. Maybe last decade it was good enough to introduce 10 new products to get one winner—and take a year or two or three to develop them. But the machine is speeding up. Next year, or the year after, we're going to need two—or three or four, or 10— successful products; and we'll need to be able to develop them in weeks, not years.

We've studied companies with effective new product development processes, and we've isolated 12 "success factors"...common traits among the successful companies:

1) A customer focus is in place. This means more than words on a framed "Mission Statement" hanging over the receptionist's desk. Successful product development companies understand the difference between customer wants and customer needs. They focus on solving customer problems, rather than focusing on what they like, can or want to do.

2) Successful companies plan before doing. It's easy to spot the unsuccessful companies—they're the ones whose whole process is caught up in the "re's"—redo, redesign, rework, revise. The winners invest the time up front to carefully select the projects on which to focus their scarce and valuable resources, then clearly define the product before starting to design.

3) An effective idea filtering system is in place. Money and resources are spent on the ideas with the greatest chance of succeeding as products. Successful companies stack the deck in their favor. The gate between the Needs Phase and the Feasibility Phase is strongly manned.

4) Resources and needs are balanced. Successful companies don't overload the pipeline. The next idea doesn't leave the Needs Phase until resources are available.

5) New product development is a company-wide job. Successful companies aren't caught up in departmental silos. Individuals on the Product Development Review Board and members of the Product Development Teams clearly understand their roles are to maximize the effectiveness of the new product development

process, not maximize the performance of their functional department.

6) A greater emphasis is placed on the Definition Phase. Only well-defined products reach the Design Phase. Successful companies refuse to commit design resources until everyone clearly understands what is being designed.

7) There's very little change in product definition in the Design Phase.

8) Process and products are designed in parallel. The old paradigm of the serial process has been superseded. Quality and manufacturability are designed in from day one.

9) Specific gates are established, providing pre-determined go/no-go points in the process.

10) Specific measurements are established for the quality of the new product development process. Successful companies can quantify what they mean by a quality new product development process, and faithfully track the process performance.

11) The companies communicate in common, customer-based terminology. Products are not described in "tech-speak" or "sales-speak," but in "customer-speak."

12) A tough leader is at the helm—someone is in charge of seeing that the methodology is followed.

MAP incorporates these 12 success factors into a single, tried-and-true process. MAP isn't product-specific. It can be used for products or services and has been used for such diverse new products as electronic equipment and consumer magazines. The real beauty of the MAP process, however, is that it doesn't require huge sums of money, new software and hardware or two new vice presidents to implement. Instead, with this book as your guide, you can get started almost immediately.

First Steps

Implementing the MAP process isn't particularly complicated, but it does require two elements that are sometimes in short supply—understanding and buy-in. Everyone in the company needs to understand the fundamentals of the MAP process and what their role in that process is. And, even more important, there needs to be a consensus—a buy-in—that everyone is going to follow the MAP, so to speak. A map can outline a route, but, ultimately, a map is only as good as the people following it.

Six basic steps complete the implementation process:

1) Make sure there is a company-wide understanding of both the need for and the dynamics of the MAP process.

2) Establish an education program aimed at answering questions about the process and helping people buy into the process. Like any process, MAP can't be shoved from the top down.

3) Write a new product development policy. (See the sample Policy in the Appendix. Note that the written policy only comes after education.)

4) Establish the Product Development Review Board (PDRB) to control the flow of new products.

5) Now you're ready to inventory all the current products in development. What phase are they in? (See the Appendix for an example of a New Product Development report that can be used to track the status and progress of all projects.) Be especially vigilant about products in some part of the Definition Phase— don't allow any products into design that might perpetuate the already existing problems.

6) Start the process. Put the gates in place. Schedule the PDRB meetings for the next six months, then call the first meeting!

When skating over thin ice, wrote Ralph Waldo Emerson, our salvation is in our speed. The marketplace of the future is going to be thin ice. It does us no good to be able to quickly tailor a service or manufacture a product if we don't have enough services and products to tailor or manufacture. If we can feed our own machines, however, we are in the best of all positions, with the ability to constantly raise our customers' expectations, then meet those expectations.

MAP Process Report

NEW PRODUCT DEVELOPMENT REPORT

This is a sample of the report produced each month that identifies the projects at each phase and communicates the performance of both the MAP process and each individual project. This is a highly confidential report and distribution is very strictly controlled.

CONTENTS

This is the index of the report:

SECTION 1. NEEDS

This section is a perpetual list of customer problems that have been identified. These represent potential opportunities to create products or services. Read Chapter 5 for a detailed discussion of the NEEDS LIST. Listed below are some examples of items that would typically be on the Needs List:

1. SMOKE STACK EMISSIONS DO NOT MEET THE NEXT STAGE OF CLEAN AIR REGULATIONS
2. FUEL COST IS VARIABLE AND CAN BE HIGH
3. INDEPENDENT POWER PRODUCERS CAN GENERATE POWER AT LOWER COST
4. ELECTRICITY DEMAND IS CYCLICAL AND VARIES AS MUCH AS 4 TO 1
5. UNSCHEDULED POWER OUTAGES ARE A LARGE PROBLEM
6. EQUIPMENT IS OLD AND OPERATING BEYOND DESIGN LIFE AT MANY POWER PLANTS

SECTION 2. FEASIBILITY

This section list the projects that have passed the Needs Gate and are being studied to determine the feasibility and wisdom of proceeding. Listed below is an example. Read Chapter 6 for a detailed discussion of the Feasibility Phase.

1. FUEL EFFICIENT BOILER

SECTION 3. DEFINITION

Projects that have passed the Feasibility Gate are listed in this section. Schedule performance for the individual product being defined is tracked. Listed below is an example. Read Chapter 7 for a detailed discussion of the Definition Phase.

BOILER EMISSIONS MONITOR

	ESTIMATED COMPLETION DATE	ACTUAL COMPLETION DATE
DEFINITION STARTED		12 FEB
DEFINITION COMPLETED	29 JUNE	

SECTION 4.   DESIGN

Projects that have passed the Design Gate are listed in this section. Schedule performance for the individual product being designed is tracked. Listed below is an example; read Chapter 8 for a detailed discussion of the Design Phase.

ELECTRONIC BOILER CONTROL

	ESTIMATED COMPLETION DATE	ACTUAL COMPLETION DATE
DEFINITION STARTED		15 JULY
DEFINITION COMPLETED	27 NOV	15 JAN
DESIGN COMPLETION	24 OCT	
PROJECT COST	$240,000	

SECTION 5: PERFORMANCE TO PLAN

This section compares the actual performance to plan of the development process and the product for each individual project. The project performance data is listed first and the product data follows.

BOILER MAINTENANCE SOFTWARE (this is the product that has been developed and passed the Design Gate)

PROJECT DATA

	PLAN	ACTUAL
DEFINITION STARTED		29 JUNE
DEFINITION COMPLETION	15 OCT	2 NOV
DESIGN COMPLETION	3 AUG	17 OCT
DEVELOPMENT COST	$150,000	$173,000

PRODUCT QUALITY DATA
    SUSTAINING COST

Year 1	$21,452
Year 2	$18,312
Year 3	$11,827
Year 4	
Year 5	

New Product Quality
Summary of all new products YTD

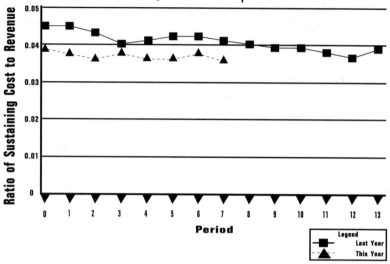

REVENUE DOLLARS

	PLAN	ACTUAL
Year 1	$375,000	$536,300
Year 2	$375,000	$484,400
Year 3	$450,000	$395,200
Year 4	$600,000	
Year 5	$300,000	

Revenue/Development $
Accumulated ratio revenue / develop $

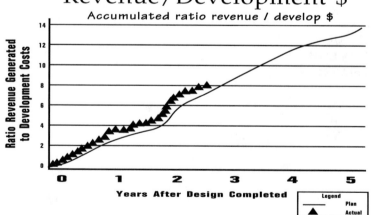

AVERAGE SALES PRICE			MANUFACTURED COST		
	PLAN	ACTUAL		PLAN	ACTUAL
Year 1	$200.00	$202.37	Year 1	$100.00	$116.21
Year 2	$200.00	$193.76	Year 2	$ 95.00	$ 98.53
Year 3	$200.00	$198.59	Year 3	$ 90.00	$ 89.74
Year 4	$190.00		Year 4		$ 85.00
Year 5	$185.00		Year 5		$ 85.00

SECTION 6. NEW PRODUCT DEVELOPMENT PROCESS MEASUREMENTS

This section provides data to measure the quality or effectiveness of MAP. These are not measures of individual projects. These are measures of the combined performance of all projects and products. Read Chapter 12 for a more complete discussion of these measurements.

% of Sales from New Products

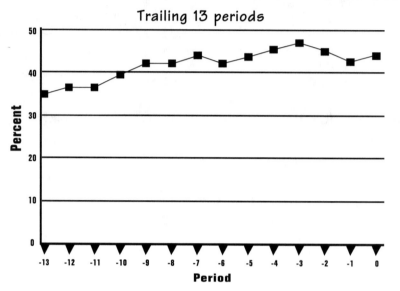

Average Product Design Time

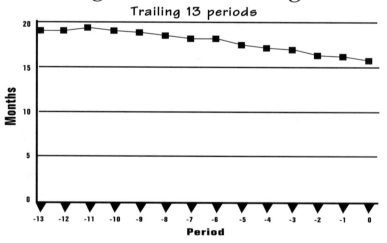

Revenue Generated by New Products

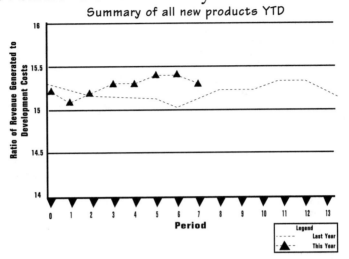

Summary of all new products YTD

Ratio of Revenue Generated to Development Costs

Period

Legend
- - - - Last Year
▲ This Year

Average Product Definition Time

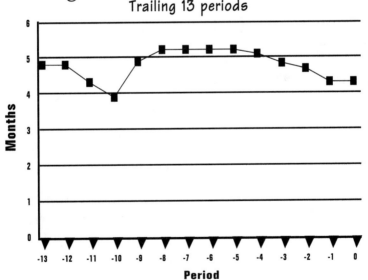

Trailing 13 periods

Months

Period

MAP Policy

1.0 PURPOSE

1.1 To provide objectives, responsibilities, and general information to guide the MAP process.

2.0 SCOPE

2.1 This procedure applies to all XXXXXXXX Corporation employees.

3.0 REFERENCE DOCUMENTS

User's Requirements Guidelines

4.0 PROCEDURE

4.1 Introduction
The new product development process is difficult, but the company's well being is determined by how well it is done. Deciding which market place needs to pursue, defining the products and services to fulfill the needs, designing the product,

and launching the product or service are the four main facets of new product development. The Product Development Policy provides objectives, responsibilities, and general information to guide the process.

4.2 PRODUCT DEVELOPMENT OBJECTIVES

4.2.1 Product Development efforts must result in products that are successful in the market place. Occasionally, a product development effort may be an essential step in long term success and not immediately successful in the market place. This exception must be a minority of the activity and well thought out.

4.2.2 New products must provide the customer value. Not all spoken wants are actually needs, and not all needs are clearly understood by the customers. New product planning must determine what actual needs to pursue.

4.2.3 New products must be timely and defect free. The average development cycle time for new products must be XX months or less. There will always be more possible product features than we can reasonably handle in a quality, timely product development effort. Therefore, new products will be introduced without all possible features incorporated. As suggested enhancements come up during the project, the project manager can incorporate them if it can be done without compromising the quality, timeliness, and cost of the project. Otherwise, it requires authorization of Product Development Review Board (PDRB) to make a change in the users requirements during the design phase. Enhancements that are not made during the product development project will be kept on an "enhancement list," and prioritized, reviewed and incorporated if appropriate during the introduction phase of the product.

4.2.4 Research and Development expenditures will be planned at a XX% of the sales rate. Personnel, which is the major expenditure in R&D, will be budgeted during the annual business planning process at a level that will result in the desired expenditure rate. The functional managers will then manage to the established budget. Projects will be started when resources are available. There will always be more ideas than can be executed with existing resources and one of the toughest decisions will be which ideas should be developed. Our success will be determined by how well we choose which things we will do and how efficiently we use the resources.

4.2.5 Marketing expenditures will be planned at a XX% of sales rate. The concepts and comments made about R&D expenditures also apply to marketing expenditures.

4.2. 6 Product development is to introduce enough successful new products that will result in XX% of sales revenue from products introduced in the last X years.

4.2.7 Hardware products should achieve a XX% gross margin within X years of product release, and software products should achieve XX% gross margin within X years of product release.

4.2.8 The usability, quality, productivity, serviceability must be designed into the product in the first place. Stated in another way, the business processes and the product are to be developed at the same time. Product development is a company wide effort involving all areas. Manufacturing, Sales, Marketing, Product Service, Quality Assurance, Finance, and Engineering must be involved from the beginning (i.e., during the definition phase). The product should be "done right the first time" so sustaining cost should not exceed XX% of the product's sales revenue.

4.3 PRODUCT DEVELOPMENT METHODOLOGY

4.3.1 Product Development Methodology will be controlled by the Product Development Review Board. Requested changes will be handled as a agenda item during the regularly scheduled meeting.

4.3.2 The Product Development Review Board is the authorizing entity for all product development (including service product development) efforts that exceed $XXX in total expenditures. Projects with expenditures of less than $XXX can be authorized by Custom Products Manager or department Vice Presidents.

4.3.3 The amount of R&D resources will be determined by the percent of sales goals. The product development planning process will simply allocate the use of those resources. The resources that are considered part of R&D are the same that contribute to the R&D cost in the companies financial statement. The R&D costs (direct labor, overhead, material and direct purchased project goods and services) will originate from all our facilities. Additionally, the Project Managers may authorize other organizations to support their R&D project.

4.3.4 The Product Development Process is composed of five phases. The phases are:
> Needs
> Feasibility
> Definition
> Design
> Launch

4.3.5 The needs phase is a perpetual process of learning about and understanding customers and their needs. At certain times during this never ending journey, decisions are made as to what customer needs should be pursued. These points in the journey are when new product projects are started. New projects will be started only when sufficient resources are available. Resources can become available by completion of a previous project, a new resource being added to the company, or the cancellation of an existing project. Only the Product Development Review Board can cancel an existing project.

4.3.6 The feasibility phase begins when a need to pursue is selected by PDRB. The feasibility phase is 4 weeks long. The mission in the feasibility phase is to quickly determine if there is any obvious problems with the project. If there are significant problems that will prevent the project from being completed it should be stopped before the resources for the full product definition effort are expended. This first step in risk, is a multi-functional effort under the direction of the team leader.

4.3.7 The definition process begins when the Product Development Review Board directs the project to be moved from the feasibility phase to the definition phase. A new product should be defined in XX months or less. The definition due date for any given project is defined by the Engineering Manager during the feasibility phase. The definition cycle ends when the Product Development Review Board approves the project to move into the design phase or decides to discontinue the project.

Detailed definitions are coordinated by the project manager and are done outside of the review board meetings. The standard of performance for the project manager is "no surprises during the design and launch of the product."

Tools like design criteria will not be used as the primary definition. The definition will be presented in terms that promote communications and a conceptual understanding of the product. Product will be defined in users terms. There is a separate guideline document in Engineering that defines "Users Requirements" in more detail.

The business processes that are required to competitively sell, manufacture, deliver and service the product will be defined at the same time the product is defined. The detailed definition of new processes will be done outside the review board meetings. The definition and impact will be communicated and coordinated by the functional department manager (i.e., the Manufacturing Manager will handle the manufacturing processes.) The standard of performance will be "no surprises during the design and launch of the product."

4.3.8 The product design phase is to be XX months or less. The design cycle time is estimated in the users requirements and approved by the Product Development Review Board as part of the product definition activity. The business processes required to sell, manufacture, deliver, and service the product will be designed at the same time the product is designed.

4.3.9 The launch phase begins when the project team determines that the product is defect free. During the launch phase the required resources from the various functional departments, including engineering, are made available to support the product and insure success.

4.4 PRODUCT DEVELOPMENT REVIEW BOARD

4.4.1 This group used to be called the Proposal Review Board. Along with the name change there is a role change. In the past, the review board has managed the detailed definition of the new products features and functions. The new review board will manage the overall fit of the product proposals with the strategy and tactics of the company. The review board will also determine the advisability of funding a project based on the merits of the user requirements. The trend is to get the Product Development Review Board to manage at more macro level and to get the Project Managers to micro manage the projects.

The review board will meet every four weeks. The meetings will be scheduled one year in advance and attendance is mandatory. The product development report and an agenda for the meeting will be distributed one week (5 working days) in advance of the meeting. Prior to the review board meeting, there are several meetings to gather information and get prepared. These advance meetings are outlined under the responsibilities of the individual review board members. The permanent members of the review board are the President, V.P. Sales and Marketing, V.P. Manufacturing and Product Development, and the Marketing Manager.

4.4.2 The voting members of the Product Development Review Board must actively stay in contact with the customers. This is usually accomplished by spending at least XX days per year visiting customers and attending customer related functions within the company's facilities.

4.4.3 The attenders and their responsibilities are:

4.4.3.1 PRESIDENT: Assures that the product development efforts are consistent with the company philosophy, objectives, strategy, and tactics. Uses information gathered with current and past contact with customers and business associations to review and comment on product definitions. Is a voting member in the product selection and project authorization process.

4.4.3.2 VICE PRESIDENT SALES & MARKETING: Assures that the product development efforts are supportive of the sales and marketing objectives. Uses information gathered with current and past contact with customers and sales force to review and comment on product definitions and strategic issues. Provides revenue projections (which will include pricing and volume information) for all new product developments. Manages the flow of new product information to the field/market place. Is a voting member in the product selection and project authorization process.

4.4.3.3 VICE PRESIDENT MANUFACTURING AND PRODUCT DEVELOPMENT: Manages the overall product development methodology. Prepares agendas for the review meetings and provides minutes of the meetings. Assures that product development projects are consistent with the resources and capabilities of manufacturing and engineering. Coordinates the technology strategy and tactics. Is responsible to facilitate communication on pertinent technological developments. Is a voting member in the product selection and project authorization process.

4.4.3.4 MARKETING MANAGER: Coordinates the product strategy and tactics. Is responsible to facilitate communication on strategy, tactics, and competitive threats communications. The voting members should not be surprised by information on these issues during review board meetings. Assures that product development projects are consistent with marketing resources. Is a voting member in the product selection and project authorization process.

4.4.3.5 ENGINEERING MANAGER: Coordinates the engineering resources and manages the engineering design methodology. Attends the meeting to gather information used to coach the project managers and give them an overview of the company direction. Presents a report on the status and availability of engineering resources. Attends all meetings but is not a voting member. Coaches project managers on the best way to interface with the review board. The Engineering Manager gives PDRB 4 weeks advanced notice when a resource is becoming available so they can prepare to select a need to pursue.

4.4.3.6 MANUFACTURING MANAGER: Coordinates the manufacturing resource and is responsible for and coordinates the "design for manufacturability" methodology. Attends the meeting to gather information used to coach and advise the Production Unit Managers and give them overview of the company direction. Presents a report on the status of the available manufacturing resources and the progress of process issues related to product development projects. Attends all meetings but is not a voting member.

4.4.3.7 CORPORATE PRODUCT SERVICE MANAGER: Provides a Gatekeeping function on advances in service technology, methodology and market expectations worldwide. Ensures that all service issues are considered in the definition phase of product development. Ensures that all CPS responsibilities as described in the Product Support Plan are achieved. Attends all PDRB meetings to represent the service organizations. Is not a voting member.

4.4.3.8 VICE PRESIDENT FINANCE: Provides a status report on the financial impact of product development efforts, and a year to date performance summary of product development performance to goals. Attends meeting a least quarterly.

4.4.3.9 QUALITY ASSURANCE MANAGER: Provides quality data on the current products and processes. Insures that quality issues that need to be addressed are properly outlined in the user requirements. Attends the meeting to gather information used to coach and advise the quality assurance personnel and give them an overview of company activities.

4.4.3.10 PROJECT MANAGERS: Coordinates on a company wide basis the detailed definition of the product to be developed. This is accomplished by development of a user's requirements and all the materials required (simulators, mechanical models, etc.) to convey the definition of the product to the review board. Arranges to be on the agenda and attends the review board meetings when necessary. Distributes written material at least 5 days in advance to the review board members. Presents project information and answers questions. Prepares project schedules and budgets that are used to determine if a project should be continued. The same schedules and budgets are used as measures to determine the performance of the development team.

4.4.3.11 MARKETING SPECIALISTS: Arranges to be on the same agenda as the associated project manager. Distributes written material at least 5 days in advance to review board members. Familiarizes the review board with the market place being addressed. Presents project marketing and sales plans and answers questions. Prepares sales revenue projections that are used to determine if a project should be continued. The projections are later used to determine the effectiveness of the product development efforts

4.4.3.12 CORPORATE COUNSEL: Corporate Counsel facilitates prudent activities on patents, intellectual property rights, legal position in the market place, and product liability.

4.5 REPORTING AND MEASUREMENTS

4.5.1 A new product development report will be issued every 4 weeks in advance of the Product Development Review Board meeting. The report will provide a summary of the status of all projects currently in progress or in their first five years of sales. If a project is canceled it will so noted in one report and then removed before the next report. The report will provide quality, timeliness, and cost measurements.

The measurements in the product development report will cover measurements of individual projects and measurements of the overall product development process.

The product development report will be used to communicate with the Board of Directors and the most recent report will be included in the Board of Directors information package.

Index